THE
OLDER BEGINNER
ORGAN COURSE

by James Bastien

CONSULTANT: Ivyle Lederer

The Bastien Older Beginner Organ Library

PREFACE

The **OLDER BEGINNER ORGAN COURSE** leads the student step by step through basic keyboard fundamentals. Each book contains original music and carefully selected familiar music to provide an enjoyable learning experience. A functional approach is used allowing the student to play and harmonize melodies from the beginning. Multi-key reading is introduced gradually through the course.

Registration is largely a matter of personal taste and is dependent on the resources available on various makes of organs. Therefore, the suggested registrations in the course are intended as guides. The student should consult the organ manufacturer's owner's manual frequently to become familiar with the various possibilities available. The student should experiment with different registrations and write in (in pencil) those which sound best on his or her instrument.

For optimum results the **OLDER BEGINNER ORGAN COURSE, LEVEL 1** is designed to be used simultaneously with its companion book **MUSICIANSHIP FOR THE OLDER BEGINNER ORGANIST, LEVEL 1.** Theory, technic and sight reading materials are presented comprehensively in this book.

Complete coordination of materials designed to be used in conjunction with this book are listed below.

Published by Kjos West.
Distributed by Neil A. Kjos Music Company.
National Order Desk, 4382 Jutland Dr., San Diego, CA 92117

ISBN 0-8497-5300-7

CONTENTS

UNIT 1

- • **INTRODUCING THE ORGAN**
- • **MANUALS AND PEDALS**
- • **THE MUSICAL ALPHABET**
- • **RHYTHM IN MUSIC**
- • **C MAJOR FIVE FINGER POSITION**
- • **C AND G MAJOR CHORDS**

INTRODUCING THE ORGAN

There are two basic types of organs: SPINET organs and CONSOLE organs.

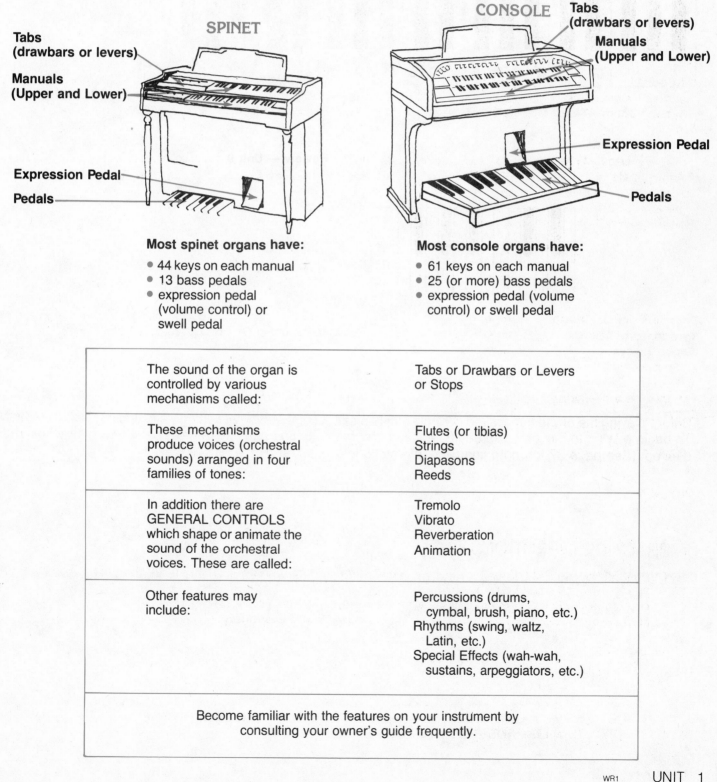

SPINET

Tabs (drawbars or levers)

Manuals (Upper and Lower)

Expression Pedal

Pedals

CONSOLE

Tabs (drawbars or levers)

Manuals (Upper and Lower)

Expression Pedal

Pedals

Most spinet organs have:

- • 44 keys on each manual
- • 13 bass pedals
- • expression pedal (volume control) or swell pedal

Most console organs have:

- • 61 keys on each manual
- • 25 (or more) bass pedals
- • expression pedal (volume control) or swell pedal

The sound of the organ is controlled by various mechanisms called:	Tabs or Drawbars or Levers or Stops
These mechanisms produce voices (orchestral sounds) arranged in four families of tones:	Flutes (or tibias) Strings Diapasons Reeds
In addition there are GENERAL CONTROLS which shape or animate the sound of the orchestral voices. These are called:	Tremolo Vibrato Reverberation Animation
Other features may include:	Percussions (drums, cymbal, brush, piano, etc.) Rhythms (swing, waltz, Latin, etc.) Special Effects (wah-wah, sustains, arpeggiators, etc.)
Become familiar with the features on your instrument by consulting your owner's guide frequently.	

MANUALS AND PEDALS

The organ has two MANUALS (keyboards) and one set of PEDALS. Notice that the arrangement of the long keys (white) and the short raised keys (black) are similar on the manuals and pedals. The short keys (black) are grouped in sets of twos and threes.

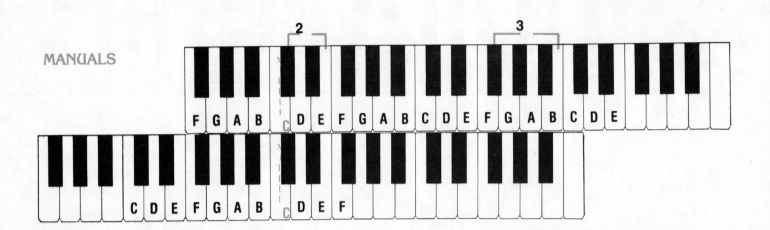

MANUALS

PEDALS

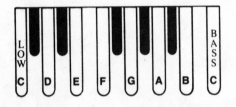

REGISTRATION

Before playing the organ the desired controls must be set. A combination of settings is called a REGISTRATION. To begin playing in this unit, use any 8' voice on the manuals and pedals. Tremolo or vibrato may be used as desired. (See page 37 for more complete information on registration.)

PRACTICE DIRECTIONS

1. Play all the sets of two black keys on both manuals, first with your Right Hand, then with your Left Hand.
2. Play all the sets of three black keys on both manuals, first with your Right Hand, then with your Left Hand.

You are ready to begin a new book in the **OLDER BEGINNER ORGAN LIBRARY —
Musicianship for the Older Beginner Organist, Level 1.**

THE MUSICAL ALPHABET

The MUSICAL ALPHABET names the white keys on the keyboard. The same seven letters (A, B, C, D, E, F, G) are used over and over.

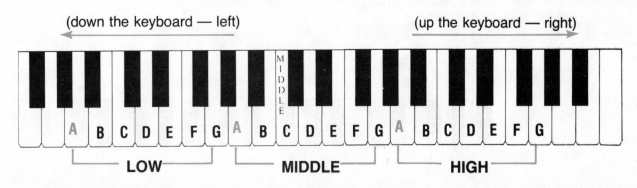

PRACTICE DIRECTIONS

1. Play the musical alphabet BOTH forward (up the keyboard) and backward (down the keyboard) in different places on the keyboard (low, middle, high). Use the second finger (either hand) for playing the seven tones; say the alphabet letter names aloud as you play.
2. Using the set of two black keys as a guide, find C, D, E on the manuals. Play all the groups of C, D, E on both manuals, first with your Right Hand, then with your Left Hand. Play with any three adjacent fingers.
3. Using the set of two black keys as a guide, find C, D, E on the pedals. Play C, D, E with your Left Foot (toe).
4. Follow the same procedure using the set of three black keys to find and play all the groups of F, G, A, B on the manuals and pedals.
5. Using the black key groups as a guide, find and play individual white keys on the manuals and pedals:
   The white key between the two black keys is D. Play all the D's on the organ.
   The white key to the left of the two black key group is C. Play all the C's on the organ.
   The white key to the right of the three black key group is B. Play all the B's on the organ.
6. Follow the same procedure with each individual white key. MEMORIZE the location of each white key name.

FINGER NUMBERS

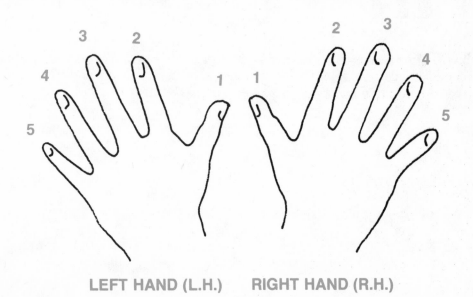

LEFT HAND (L.H.)   RIGHT HAND (R.H.)

PRACTICE DIRECTIONS
Say these finger numbers aloud, moving the corresponding fingers up and down. Learn these finger numbers so they become automatic.

RHYTHM IN MUSIC

Every piece has a pattern of short and long tones. The combination of short and long tones is called RHYTHM.

QUARTER NOTE	HALF NOTE	WHOLE NOTE
♩ (one clap)	♩ (clap - shake)	𝅝 (clap - shake - shake - shake)
Count: "quarter"	Count: "half - note"	Count: "Whole - note - hold - it"
or	or	or
Count: 1	Count: 1 - 2	Count: 1 - 2 - 3 - 4

PRACTICE DIRECTIONS

1. Clap and count the following note values aloud. Use either counting system (or any alternate system).
2. Play any white key on the manuals or pedals in this rhythm. Count aloud as you play. (Have your instructor show you how to use the Rhythm Unit with this rhythm pattern.)

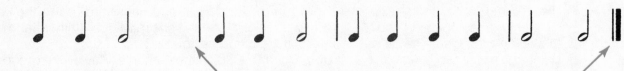

Count: "quarter quarter half - note"
or
Count: 1   1   1 - 2

A BAR LINE divides the rhythm into MEASURES.

A DOUBLE BAR is used at the end.

C MAJOR FIVE FINGER POSITION

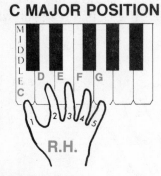

C MAJOR POSITION

R.H.

- When reading music, KEEP YOUR EYES ON THE BOOK.
- Play with a LEGATO touch. Connect the tones smoothly.

PRACTICE DIRECTIONS

1. Find the position for your Right Hand.
2. Play and sing the FINGER NUMBERS aloud.
3. Play again and COUNT the rhythm aloud.
4. Play again and SING the letter names of the notes aloud.

ELECTRONIC ORGANS
UPPER: Flutes (Tibias) 8′ 4′
TREM: On (Fast)
VIB: On (Full)

Warm-Up

DRAWBAR ORGANS *
No. 5

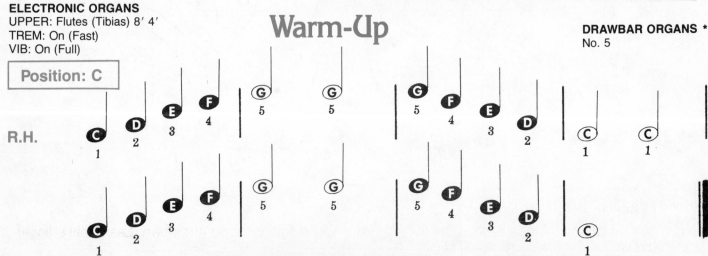

Position: C

R.H.

*Refer to the SUGGESTED ORGAN REGISTRATIONS on the inside back cover for all DRAWBAR ORGAN registrations.

PRACTICE DIRECTIONS

Follow the same PRACTICE DIRECTIONS given on page 8 for these two pieces.

AU CLAIR DE LA LUNE

ELECTRONIC ORGANS
UPPER: Violin 8'
VIB: On (Light or Delay)

DRAWBAR ORGANS
No. 8

Position: C

FRENCH FOLK SONG

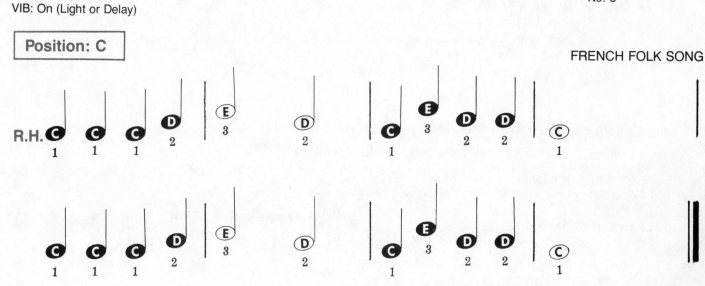

LARGO

(from the "New World Symphony")

ELECTRONIC ORGANS
UPPER: Clarinet 8'
TREM. and VIB: Off

DRAWBAR ORGANS
No. 9

Position: C

ANTONIN DVOŘÁK
(1841-1904)

> **ACCOMPANIMENT ON THE ORGAN**
> On the organ melodies are accompanied by CHORDS, PEDALS, or both together.

C AND G MAJOR CHORDS

- A CHORD is three or more tones played at the same time.

The C MAJOR CHORD and the G MAJOR CHORD
are the two chords used in this unit.

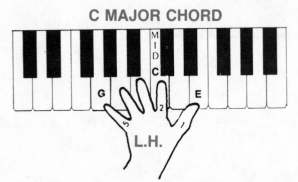
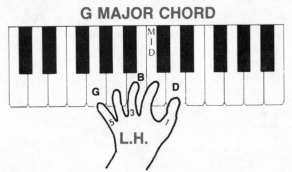

C MAJOR CHORD   **G MAJOR CHORD**

- Changing from one chord to another is called a CHORD PROGRESSION.
- A chord's name is indicated by letters called CHORD SYMBOLS.*

ELECTRONIC ORGANS LOWER: Diapason 8' Flute 8' TREM. and VIB: Off
DRAWBAR ORGANS No. 6

PRACTICE DIRECTIONS

Play the following **Chord Progression** in the rhythm given. Hold finger 5 down while playing these chords.

Chord Progression

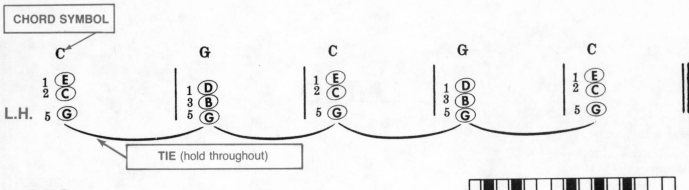

CHORD SYMBOL

TIE (hold throughout)

PEDALS
PEDALS give a foundation to chords and melodies.
The C PEDAL and the G PEDAL are the two pedals used in this unit.

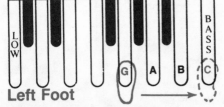

Left Foot

ELECTRONIC ORGANS PEDAL: 8'
DRAWBAR ORGANS No. 6

PRACTICE DIRECTIONS (Wear shoes!)
1. Position your Left Foot in line with G. Place your entire Right Foot on the Expression Pedal.
2. To establish a feeling for distance, play G and "walk" up to C (G, A, B, C). Play by "feel." Do NOT look at the pedals while playing.
3. Following the rhythm above (whole notes), play Bass C, G, Bass C, G, Bass C alternately.
4. Play the chords and the pedals together in the rhythm above.

*Chord symbols represent a practical form of musical shorthand. When chord symbols are printed above melodies, organists can improvise accompaniments.

PRACTICE DIRECTIONS

1. Play the Right Hand melody and pedals together. Count aloud as you play.
2. Play the Right Hand melody and Left Hand accompaniment (chords) together. Count as you play.
3. Play the melody, accompaniment, and pedals together. Count aloud as you play. (Follow this practice procedure for all succeeding pieces.)

ELECTRONIC ORGANS
UPPER: Strings 8' 4'
LOWER: Flute 8'
PEDAL: 16'
TREM: On (Fast)
VIB: On (Light/Delay)

Position: C

AU CLAIR DE LA LUNE

DRAWBAR ORGANS
No. 8

FRENCH FOLK SONG

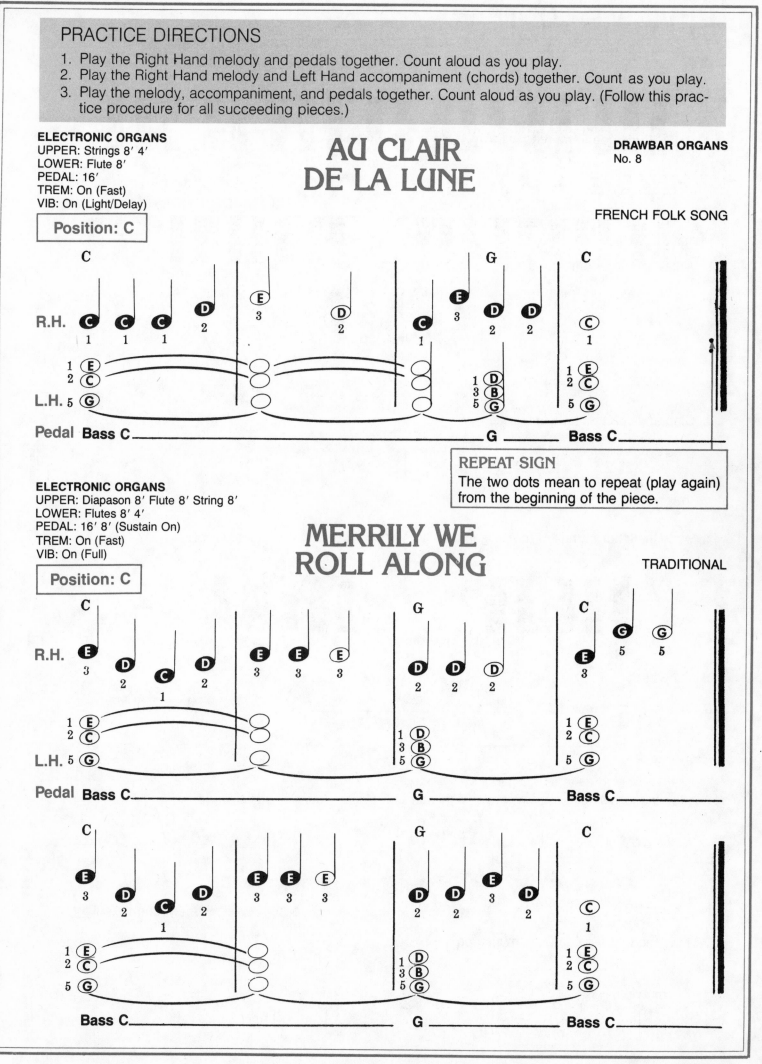

REPEAT SIGN
The two dots mean to repeat (play again) from the beginning of the piece.

ELECTRONIC ORGANS
UPPER: Diapason 8' Flute 8' String 8'
LOWER: Flutes 8' 4'
PEDAL: 16' 8' (Sustain On)
TREM: On (Fast)
VIB: On (Full)

Position: C

MERRILY WE ROLL ALONG

TRADITIONAL

REVIEW — UNIT 1

1. Write the letter name of each key marked with an X.

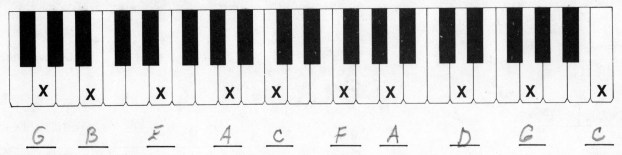

G   B   E   A   C   F   A   D   G   C

2. Write the letter names of the keys in the C Major Five Finger Position.

C D E F G A B

3. Clap and count this rhythm pattern.

4. Write the letter names of the keys in the C Major chord and the G Major chord.

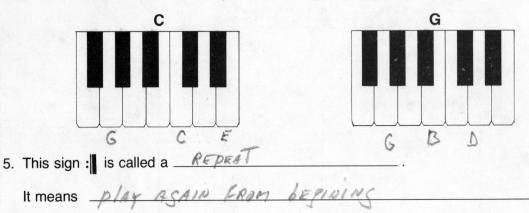

C G   C   E   **G** G   B   D

5. This sign :‖ is called a ___REPEAT___ .

   It means ___play again from begining___

6. Play the following chords in rhythm with your Left Hand. Count aloud as you play.

C   G   C

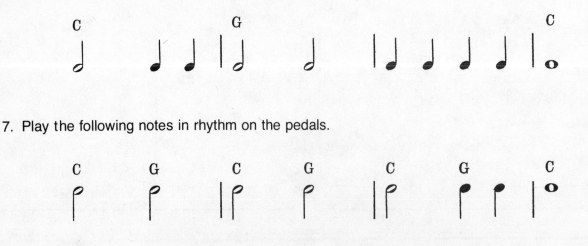

7. Play the following notes in rhythm on the pedals.

C   G   C   G   C   G   C

UNIT 2
. **BEGINNING MUSIC FACTS**

BEGINNING MUSIC FACTS

STAFFS — CLEFS

The STAFF has 5 lines and 4 spaces.

The TREBLE STAFF is indicated by a TREBLE CLEF (or G clef) sign:

The BASS STAFF is indicated by a BASS CLEF (or F clef) sign:

The Treble Staff and the Bass Staff are joined together by a brace to form the GRAND STAFF.

BRACE➤

The notes shown below are used frequently. Notice that some notes are placed on a LEGER LINE (a short line added to the staff to extend the staff).

The MELODY is written on the upper staff (treble); the ACCOMPANIMENT and PEDAL NOTES are written on the lower staff (bass).

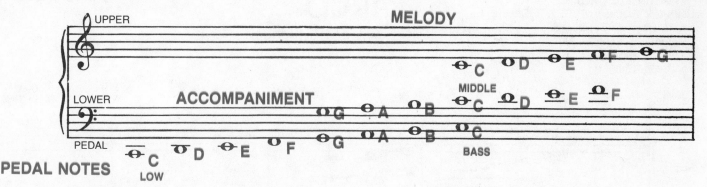

The C and G Major chords introduced in UNIT 1 are notated in the following manner:

C MAJOR CHORD   **G MAJOR CHORD**

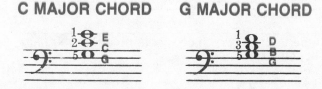

PRACTICE DIRECTIONS

1. KEEP YOUR EYES ON THE BOOK while playing.
2. Play the Right Hand melody notes shown above both forward and backward, saying the letter names of the notes aloud as you play.
3. Play the C and G Major chords shown above with your Left Hand.
4. With your Left Foot play the pedal notes shown above from the lowest C to the C above. Play back down again. Say the letter names of the notes aloud as you play.

TIME SIGNATURES

The two numbers written at the beginning of each composition make up the TIME SIGNATURE. The upper number indicates the number of beats (or counts) in a measure. The lower number indicates what kind of a note gets one beat.

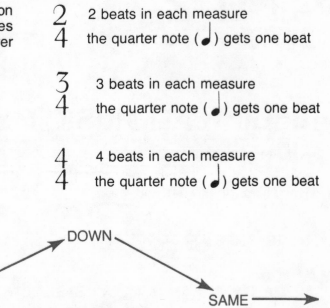

2 2 beats in each measure
4 the quarter note (♩) gets one beat

3 3 beats in each measure
4 the quarter note (♩) gets one beat

4 4 beats in each measure
4 the quarter note (♩) gets one beat

Notes on the staff move in one of three ways:
Read notes by direction.

DOWN

UP   SAME

PRACTICE DIRECTIONS*

1. Clap and count the rhythm of the Right Hand melody aloud before playing.
2. Find your position for hands and feet.
3. Keep your eyes on the book while playing.
4. Practice each part separately. SING the letter names of the notes aloud.** Next, play and COUNT the rhythm aloud.
5. Follow the practice procedure outlined on page 11.

ELECTRONIC ORGANS
UPPER: Diapason 8′ Flute 8′ Oboe 8′
LOWER: Flute 8′ String 8′
PEDAL: 16′ (Sustain On)
TREM: On (Slow/Celeste)
VIB: On (Light)

LARGO
(from the "New World Symphony")

DRAWBAR ORGANS
No. 12

ANTONIN DVOŘÁK
(1841-1904)

TIE—a curved line which connects notes on the same line or space; hold the tied notes.

*Similar practice directions should be followed throughout this book.
Drill on these notes using the **Bastien Music Flashcards.

ELECTRONIC ORGANS
UPPER: Flutes 8′ 4′ 2′ Strings 8′ 4′
LOWER: Diapason 8′ Flutes 8′ 4′ String 8′
PEDAL: 16′ 8′
TREM: On (Slow/Celeste)
VIB: Off

DRAWBAR ORGANS
No. 2

ODE TO JOY

LUDWIG VAN BEETHOVEN
(1770-1827)

ELECTRONIC ORGANS
UPPER: Flutes 16′ 4′ 2′ Reed 16′
LOWER: Diapason 8′ Flute 8′ String 8′
PEDAL: String Bass or Flute 8′ (Sustain On)
TREM. and VIB: Off
RHYTHM: Jazz Rock

DRAWBAR ORGANS
No. 6
RHYTHM: Jazz Rock

FIRST ROCK

You are ready to begin a new book — **Note Speller, Level 1.**

DOTTED HALF NOTE

𝅗𝅥. (clap - shake - shake)
Count: "Half - note - dot"
or
Count: 1 - 2 - 3

D.C. AL FINE

D.C. al Fine (abbreviation for *Da Capo al Fine,*) is a DIRECTION SIGN. It means to go back to the beginning of the piece and play to the word *Fine* (pronounced "fee-nay").

ELECTRONIC ORGANS
UPPER: Flutes 16′ 8′ 4′ Clarinet 8′
LOWER: Diapason 8′ Flute 8′
PEDAL: 16′ 8′ (Sustain On)
TREM: On (Fast)
VIB: Off
RHYTHM: Swing

DRAWBAR ORGANS
No. 11
RHYTHM: Swing

ALOUETTE

FRENCH FOLK SONG

UNIT 2   WR1

PRACTICE DIRECTIONS

Play each exercise with your Left Foot several times. Name the notes aloud as you play.

Pedal Exercise

ELECTRONIC ORGANS
UPPER: Diapason 8′ Flute 8′ String 8′
       Oboe 8′ Saxophone (or Kinura) 8′
LOWER: Flute 8′ String 8′
PEDAL: Bourdon 16′ Flute 8′ (Sustain On)
TREM: Adjust to suit the piece

DRAWBAR ORGANS
No. 5

LIGHTLY ROW

FOLK SONG

Light-ly row, light-ly row, O'er the roll-ing waves we go,

Off we go, off we go, 'Way from shore we glide.

Love-ly day out for a sail, Sun-shine spark-lin' with-out fail.

Light-ly row, light-ly row, O'er the waves we go.

rit.

RITARDANDO
rit. is the abbreviation for *ritardando*.
It means to gradually play slower.

OCTAVE SIGN 8va

The OCTAVE SIGN above the notes means to play one octave (eight notes) higher than written.

RESTS

RESTS indicate measured silence. Each note has a rest sign of the same value (same number of beats).

NOTES RESTS

Quarter Rest (1 beat)

Half Rest (2 beats)

Whole Rest (4 beats, or whole measure)

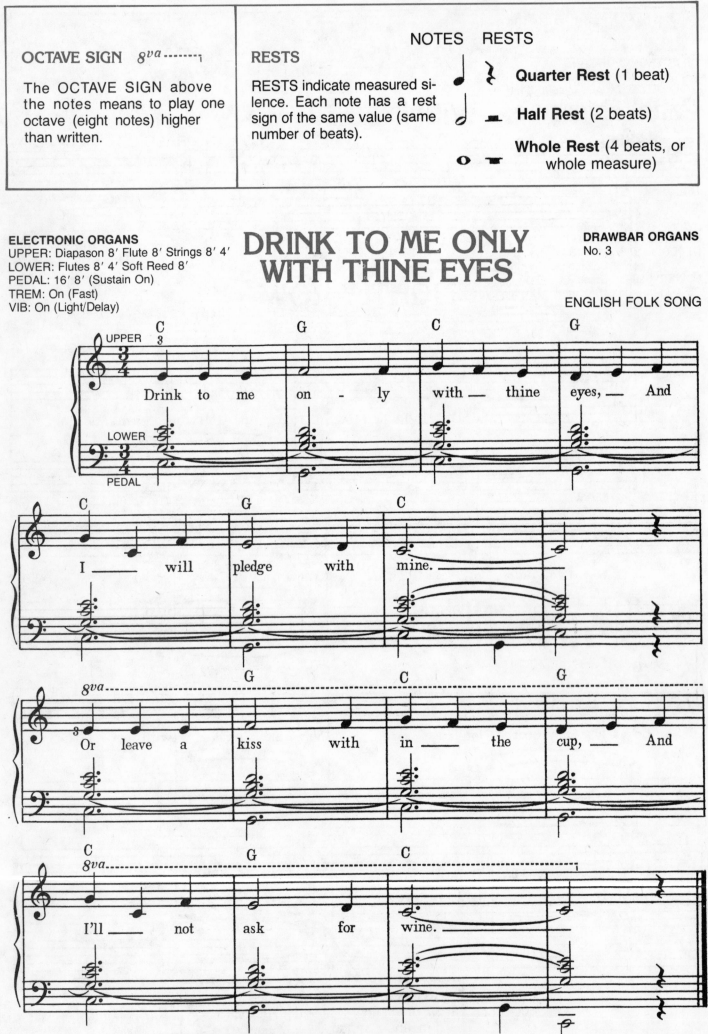

ELECTRONIC ORGANS
UPPER: Diapason 8′ Flute 8′ Strings 8′ 4′
LOWER: Flutes 8′ 4′ Soft Reed 8′
PEDAL: 16′ 8′ (Sustain On)
TREM: On (Fast)
VIB: On (Light/Delay)

DRINK TO ME ONLY WITH THINE EYES

DRAWBAR ORGANS
No. 3

ENGLISH FOLK SONG

ELECTRONIC ORGANS
UPPER: Flutes 16′ 8′ Clarinet 8′
LOWER: Diapason 8′ Flute 8′ String 8′
PEDAL: 16′ 8′ (Sustain On)
TREM: On (Fast)
VIB: Off
RHYTHM: Waltz (¾)

DRAWBAR ORGANS
No. 1
RHYTHM: Waltz (¾)

VIENNESE WALTZ

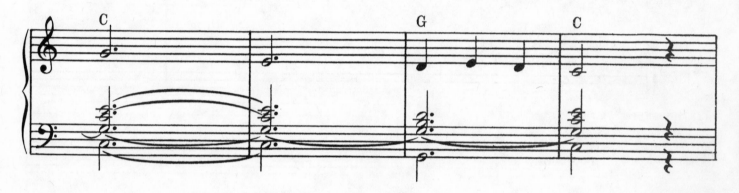

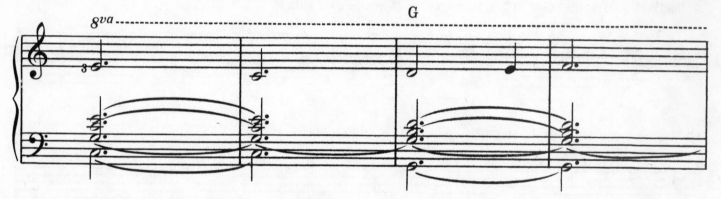

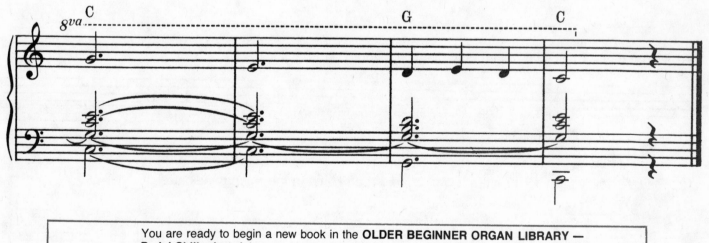

You are ready to begin a new book in the **OLDER BEGINNER ORGAN LIBRARY** —
Pedal Skills, Level 1.

REVIEW — UNIT 2

1. Draw these notes.

   a. Quarter Note   b. Half Note   c. Whole Note   d. Dotted Half Note

2. A group of 5 lines and 4 spaces is called a ___STAFF___.

3. The two numbers written at the beginning of a composition make up the ___TIME SIGNATURE___.

4. A curved line which connects notes on the same line or space is called a ___TIE___.

5. Measured silence is indicated in music by ___RESTs___.

6. This sign *8va* is called an ___OCTAVE SIGN___.

   It means ___play ONE OCTAVE higher___

7. This sign *D. C. al Fine* means ___go back TO begining play To FINE___

8. This sign *rit.* means to ___gradually play slower___

9. Name these Treble Clef notes. Play them with your Right Hand.

   G   E   F   D   E   C   E

10. Name these Bass Clef notes. Play them with your Left Hand.

    G   D   B   E   C   A   D

11. Name these Bass Clef notes. Play them with your Left Foot.

    C   G   B   C   A   E   E

12. Play the following chord progression with your Left Hand in the rhythm indicated.

UNIT 3
- **PLAYING OUT OF THE FIVE FINGER POSITION**
- **EIGHTH NOTES**
- **F MAJOR CHORD**

PLAYING OUT OF THE FIVE FINGER POSITION

MOVING THE THUMB DOWN
Often it is necessary to MOVE YOUR THUMB DOWN to play melodies extending out of the five finger position.

> **PRACTICE DIRECTIONS**
> Practice the following drill as preparation for melodies extending out of the five finger position.

Preparatory Drill

ELECTRONIC ORGANS
UPPER: Clarinet 8′ Flute 4′
LOWER: Flutes 8′ 4′
PEDAL: 16′ (Sustain On)
TREM: On (Fast)
VIB: Off

DRAWBAR ORGANS
No. 3

VALSE ROMANTIQUE

(melody 8va on repeat)

TEMPO

TEMPO is the rate of speed at which a piece is played. Usually tempo markings appear in Italian (such as *Moderato, Andante, Allegretto*). Sometimes, however, tempo markings appear in English (such as *Moderately, Slowly, Lively, Fast*). Watch for the tempo markings at the BEGINNING of the piece.

ELECTRONIC ORGANS
UPPER: Trombone 16′ Diapason 8′
LOWER: Flutes 8′ 4′ String 8′
PEDAL: 16′ 8′ (Sustain On)
TREM: On (Slow/Celeste)
VIB: On (Light)
RHYTHM: Latin

DRAWBAR ORGANS
No. 6
RHYTHM: Latin

MARY ANN

Moderato (at a moderate rate of speed)

TRADITIONAL

EIGHTH NOTES

An EIGHTH NOTE receives HALF of one beat (in a time signature where a quarter note receives one beat). One eighth note has a FLAG: ♪

EIGHTH NOTE

♪ = ½ beat

EIGHTH REST

𝄾 = ½ beat

TWO EIGHTH NOTES equal one quarter note and receive one beat. Two eighth notes are paired together with a BEAM:

TWO EIGHTH NOTES

♫ = ♩ = 1 beat

♫ (clap, clap)

Count: "Two eighths"
or
Count: 1 and

PRACTICE DIRECTIONS Clap and count the following rhythm.

Count: quarter two 8ths half — note
or
Count: 1   2 and 3 — 4

ALL ORGANS
Special Effects Solo Banjo*
(or String 8′)
RHYTHM: Fox Trot

*Refer to Owner's Manual

SKIP TO MY LOU

Lively   TRADITIONAL

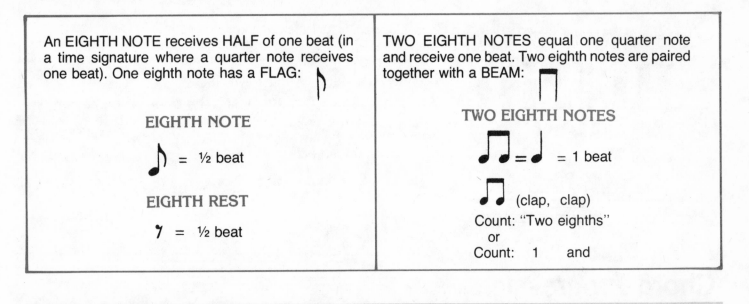

Lou, lou, skip to my lou, Lou, lou, skip to my lou,

Lou, lou, skip to my lou, Skip to my lou my dar - ling.

F MAJOR CHORD

By learning the F Major chord you will be able to harmonize many melodies.

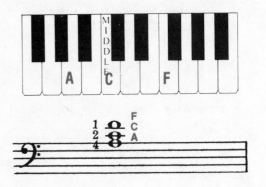

Chord Progression

Pedal Exercise

Chord Progression

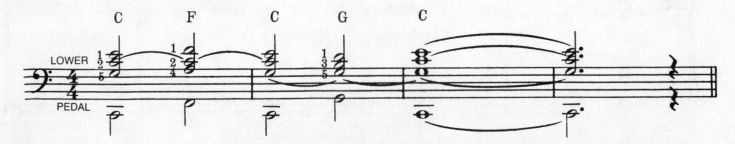

MOVING THE FIFTH FINGER UP
Often it is necessary to MOVE YOUR FIFTH FINGER UP to play melodies out of the five finger position.

PRACTICE DIRECTIONS
Practice the following drill as preparation for melodies extending out of the five finger position.

Practice the chords and pedal part for **LAVENDER'S BLUE** separately. Then play the melody and pedal part separately. Finally, play as written.

ELECTRONIC ORGANS
UPPER: Diapason 8' Flute 8' Kinura (Reed) 8'
LOWER: Flutes 8' 4'
PEDAL: 16' 8' (Sustain On)
TREM: On (Slow/Celeste)
VIB: On (Light)
RHYTHM: Waltz (¾)

DRAWBAR ORGANS
No. 10
RHYTHM: Waltz (¾)

LAVENDER'S BLUE

Moderato

ENGLISH FOLK SONG

UPBEAT

A note (or notes) which comes before the first full measure of a piece is called an UPBEAT (sometimes called a PICK-UP or ANACRUSIS). Usually the time value of the upbeat is taken from the final measure, making the final measure INCOMPLETE.

FERMATA SIGN

This sign is called a FERMATA. It means to HOLD the note (or notes) LONGER than the time value.

ELECTRONIC ORGANS
UPPER: Flutes 16′ 8′ Cello 16′ Reed 16′
LOWER: Diapason 8′ Flutes 8′ 4′
PEDAL: 16′ 8′ (Sustain On)
TREM: On (Fast)
VIB: On (Full)

DRAWBAR ORGANS
No. 1

FOR HE'S A
JOLLY GOOD FELLOW

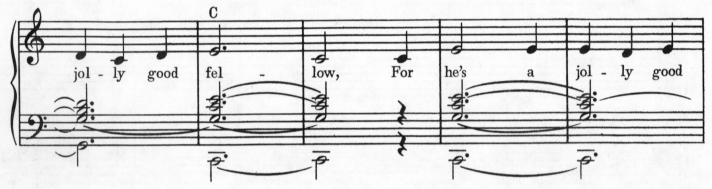

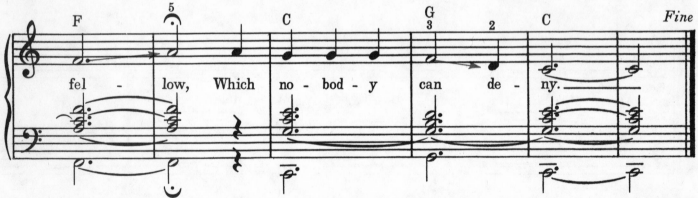

DYNAMICS

DYNAMICS are the degrees of softness and loudness with which music should be performed. Music signs are used as dynamic indicators.

SIGN	ITALIAN NAME	MEANING
p	*piano*	soft
mp	*mezzo piano*	medium soft
mf	*mezzo forte*	medium loud
f	*forte*	loud

EXPRESSION PEDAL

The volume of sound produced can be increased or decreased by the EXPRESSION PEDAL.

- TO INCREASE VOLUME:
  press TOE forward.
- TO DECREASE VOLUME:
  press HEEL down.

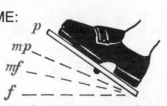

ELECTRONIC ORGANS
UPPER: Diapason 8′ Flutes 8′ 4′ Reed 8′
LOWER: Reed 8′ String 8′
PEDAL: 16′ 8′ (Sustain On)
TREM. and VIB: Off
RHYTHM: Rock Beat

DRAWBAR ORGANS
No. 6
RHYTHM: Rock Beat

ROCK ABOUT

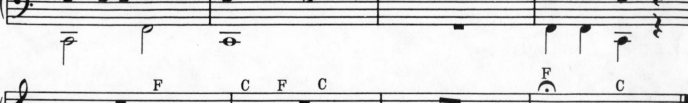

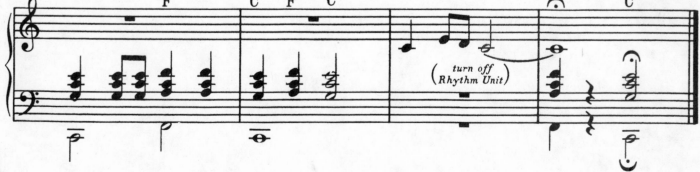

REVIEW — UNIT 3

1. Draw these notes.
   a. Dotted Half Note   b. Two Eighth Notes   c. Quarter Note

2. Name these rests.

   half   whole   QUARTER   Eighth

3. A note (or notes) which comes before the first full measure of a piece is called an _upbeat_.

4. This sign 𝄐 is called a _FERMATA_.
   It means _hold NOTES LONGER THAN TIME VALUE_.

5. Draw a note on the staff above each letter. Use whole notes. Play them with your Right Hand.

   G   Middle C   F   B below staff   D   A   E

6. Draw a note on the staff above each letter. Use whole notes. Play them with your Left Hand.

   G space   D above staff   B space   E above staff   Middle C   A line   F above staff

7. Draw a note on the staff above each letter. Use whole notes. Play them with your Left Foot.

   C space   G line   B line   C below staff   A space   F space   E below staff

8. Name these dynamic signs.

SIGN	ITALIAN NAME	MEANING
p	PIANO	SOFT
f	FORTE	Loud
mf	MEZZO FORTE	MED. Loud
mp	MEZZO PIANO	MED SOFT

9. Play the following chord progression with your Left Hand in the rhythm indicated.

   C F C   C G C   C F C   G   C

UNIT 4

- **ACCIDENTALS**
- **G7 CHORD**

ACCIDENTALS ♯ ♭ ♮

ACCIDENTALS are added signs which temporarily alter the pitch of notes. The effect of accidental signs lasts only within the measure they appear.

A SHARP sign (♯) before a note means to play the NEXT KEY to the RIGHT. The next key may be black or white.

A FLAT sign (♭) before a note means to play the NEXT KEY to the LEFT. The next key may be black or white.

The NATURAL sign (♮) is used to cancel a sharp or flat. It means to play the natural key (white key). Frequently a natural sign is used as a REMINDER in the next measure.

REMINDER

ENHARMONIC NOTATION

Tones which sound the same but look different in print are termed ENHARMONIC (F♯ — G♭). The language equivalent is "to, too, two."

The keyboard shows the enharmonic names from A to A.

ELECTRONIC ORGANS
*UPPER: Wah-Wah (Funny) or Reed 16'
LOWER: Diapason 8'
PEDAL: String Bass 8'
TREM. and VIB: Off
RHYTHM: Rock Beat

DRAWBAR ORGANS
No. 6
RHYTHM: Rock Beat

SATURDAY NIGHT

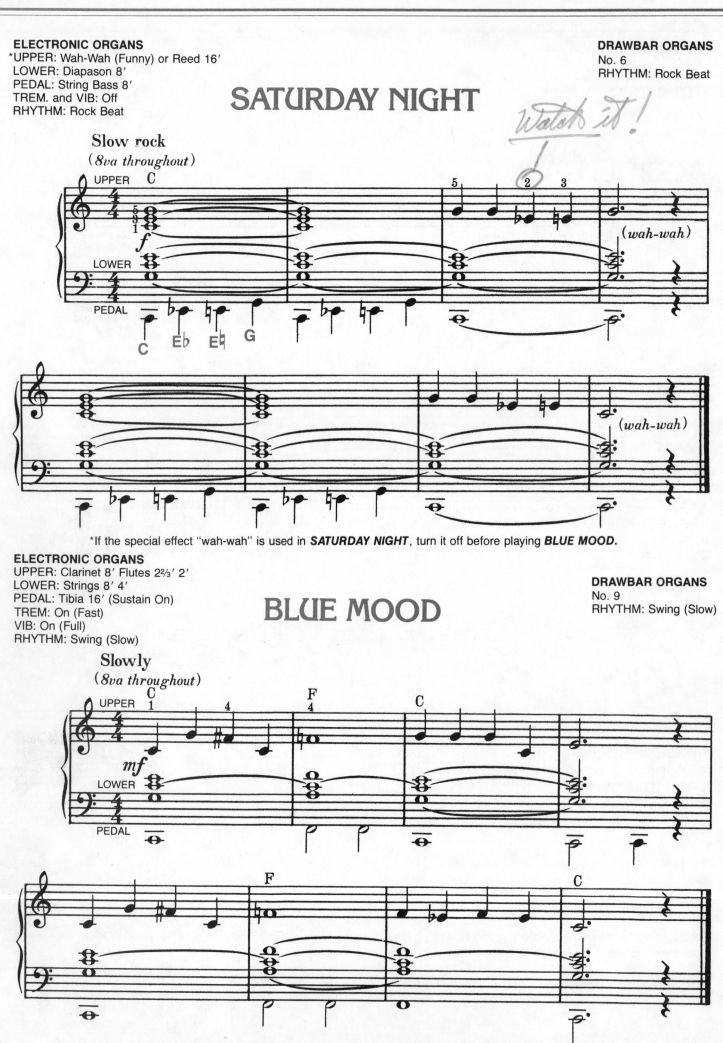

*If the special effect "wah-wah" is used in **SATURDAY NIGHT**, turn it off before playing **BLUE MOOD**.

ELECTRONIC ORGANS
UPPER: Clarinet 8' Flutes 2⅔' 2'
LOWER: Strings 8' 4'
PEDAL: Tibia 16' (Sustain On)
TREM: On (Fast)
VIB: On (Full)
RHYTHM: Swing (Slow)

DRAWBAR ORGANS
No. 9
RHYTHM: Swing (Slow)

BLUE MOOD

ELECTRONIC ORGANS
UPPER: Saxophone 8′
LOWER: Flutes 8′ 4′
PEDAL: Flute 16′ String Bass 8′
TREM. and VIB: Off
RHYTHM: Jazz Rock

DRAWBAR ORGANS
No. 10
RHYTHM: Rock

STEPPIN' OUT

ELECTRONIC ORGANS
UPPER: Flutes 16′ 8′ 4′ Strings 8′ 4′
LOWER: Diapason 8′ Reed 8′
PEDAL: 16′ 8′ (Sustain On)
TREM: On (Fast)
VIB: On (Full)
RHYTHM: Fox Trot

DRAWBAR ORGANS
No. 7
RHYTHM: Fox Trot

THE OLD GREY MARE

G7 CHORD

The G7 chord is formed by adding F to the G chord.

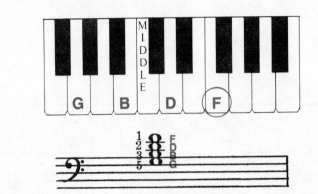

PRACTICE DIRECTIONS

Practice these **Chord Progressions** until you can play them smoothly. Play by "feel." Do NOT look at your Left Hand and Left Foot for the chord changes.

Chord Progressions

1.

(This note, D, may be omitted to facilitate playing the G7 chord.)

2.

3.

ELECTRONIC ORGANS
UPPER: Flutes 16′ 4′ 2′
LOWER: Diapason 8′ String 8′
PEDAL: 16′ 8′ (Sustain On)
TREM: On (Fast)
VIB: On (Full)
RHYTHM: Waltz (¾)

DRAWBAR ORGANS
No. 11
RHYTHM: Waltz (¾)

BEAUTIFUL, BEAUTIFUL BROWN EYES

Moderato

TRADITIONAL

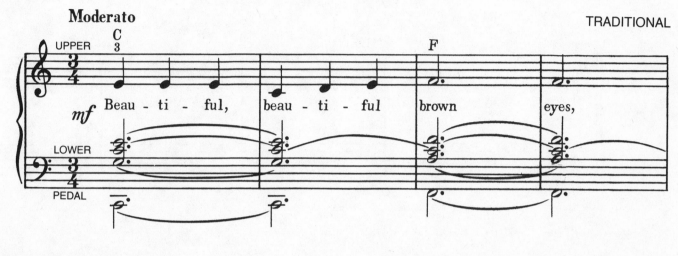

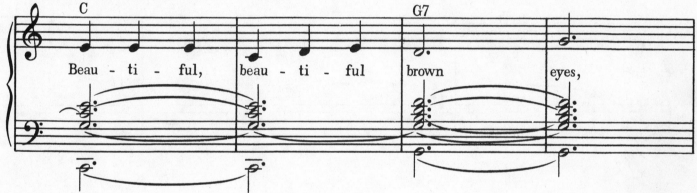

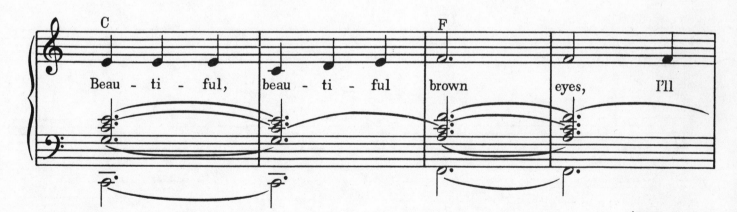

(Melody 8va on repeat)

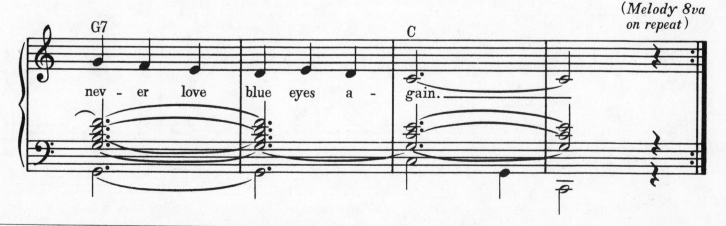

ELECTRONIC ORGANS
UPPER: Flute 8′ Diapason 8′ Reed 8′
        Strings 8′ 4′
LOWER: Flutes 8′ 4′ Reed 8′
PEDAL: 16′ 8′
TREM: On (Slow/Celeste)
VIB: On (Light) or Off

DRAWBAR ORGANS
No. 2

THEME FROM THE 9TH SYMPHONY

LUDVIG VAN BEETHOVEN
(1770-1827)

With spirit

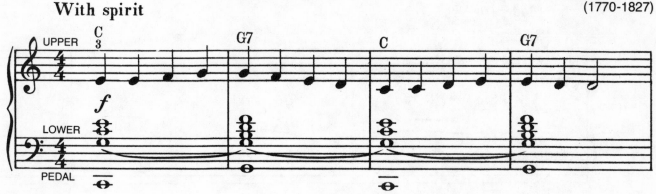

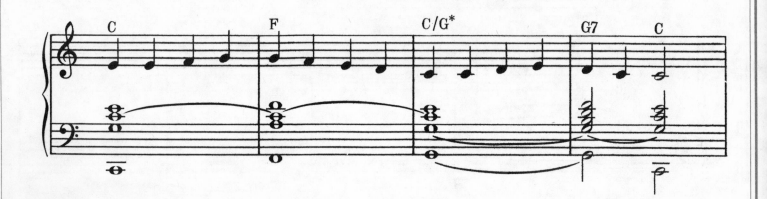

PEDAL POINT (or ORGAN POINT)
The same pedal note is held throughout the chord changes.

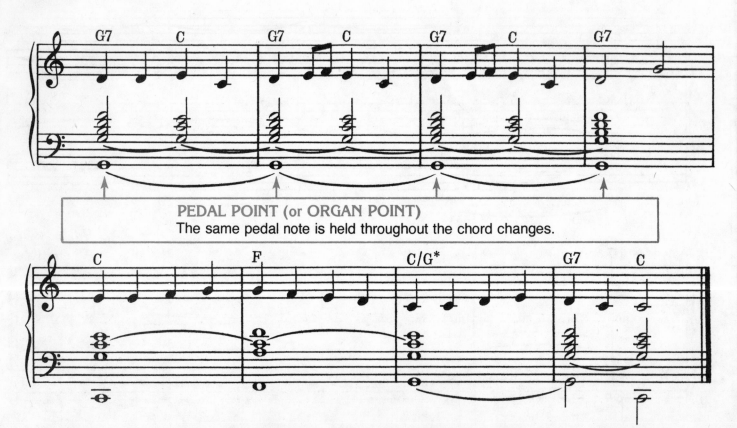

*This chord symbol is used when the pedal note is different from the chord's name. C/G = C chord with G pedal note.

PRACTICE DIRECTIONS
Practice the accompaniment parts (Left Hand and pedal) until they can be played in time with the Rhythm Unit.

ALL ORGANS
Using Registration No. 1 or Registration No. 6 as a guide, write (in pencil) a registration of your choice.*

UPPER:_____

LOWER: _____

PEDAL:_____

TREM. or VIB: _____

RHYTHM: _____

WHEN THE SAINTS GO MARCHING IN

TRADITIONAL

With spirit

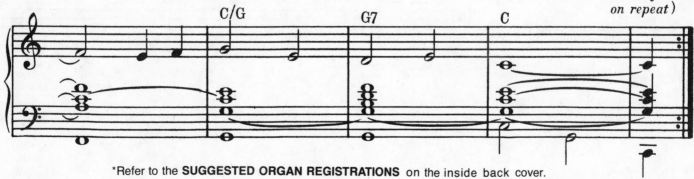

*Refer to the **SUGGESTED ORGAN REGISTRATIONS** on the inside back cover.

WR1   UNIT 4

REVIEW — UNIT 4

1. Name these sharped notes. Play them.

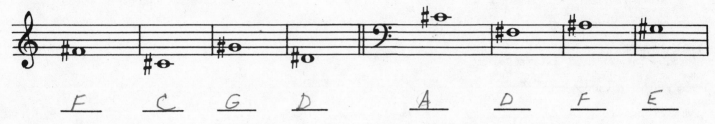

F   C   G   D   A   D   F   E

2. Name these flatted notes. Play them.

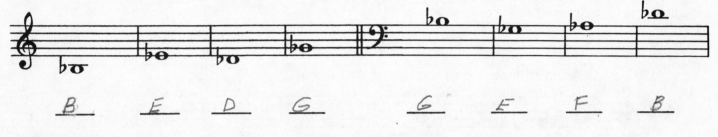

B   E   D   G   G   E   F   B

3. Name the second note in each measure. Play all the notes.

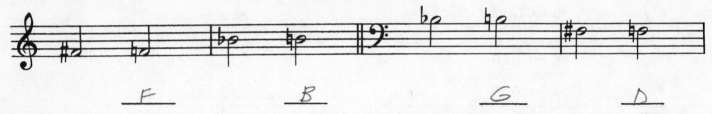

F   B   G   D

4. Name these chords. Play them with your Left Hand.

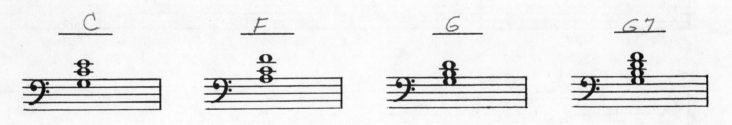

C   F   G   G7

5. Draw these chords. Play them with your Left Hand.

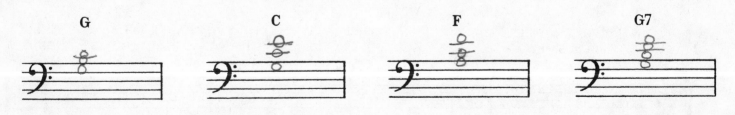

G   C   F   G7

6. Play the following chord progression with your Left Hand in the rhythm indicated.

UNIT 5

- **REGISTRATION TIPS**
- **HALF STEPS AND WHOLE STEPS**
- **C MAJOR SCALE**

REGISTRATION TIPS

UNDERSTANDING THE TERMINOLOGY

Organ terminology refers to the pipe organ. The length of the pipe determines the pitch — low or high. Long pipes produce low tones; short pipes produce high tones.

The numerals appearing on the voice controls (tabs, drawbars, levers, stops) indicate differences in pitch:

8′ (eight foot) means the **ACTUAL TONE** (the pitch that is written).

16′ (sixteen foot) means the same tone, but sounding **ONE OCTAVE LOWER** than written.

4′ (four foot) means the same tone, but sounding **ONE OCTAVE HIGHER** than written.

2′ (two foot) means the same tone, but sounding **TWO OCTAVES HIGHER** than written.

1′ (one foot) means the same tone, but sounding **THREE OCTAVES HIGHER** than written.

SELECTING A REGISTRATION

The following registration guidelines are given in general terms. Your selection will depend on the various possibilities of your instrument and your personal taste.

Before playing a piece:

1. Determine the style of the piece. Is it a Ballad, March, Hymn Tune, etc.? Try different combinations of tones which best suit the mood and style of the music.

   These suggestions will give you some ideas for several different styles:

   BALLAD:
   Flutes accompanied by Strings
   String solo accompanied by Flutes
   Reed solo accompanied by Flutes and Strings
   (Tremolo or Vibratos on)

   MARCH:
   strong Reeds accompanied by Diapasons
   (Tremolo or Vibrato on)

   HYMN TUNE:
   Combinations of Diapasons, Flutes, Strings (often played on the same manual)
   (Tremolo or Vibrato slow or off)

   POP:
   Strong Reeds accompanied by Diapasons
   (Tremolo or Vibrato on)

2. Before setting the registration begin with the Expression Pedal one-half open (mf). With one hand depress and hold a key or chord on the manual to be registered. This will enable you to hear your registration as you build it.

3. Set different families of tones with different dynamic levels on each manual. The melody should be heard clearly above the accompaniment. In addition the pedal should blend but not overpower the melody and accompaniment.

4. Tremolos or Vibratos differ widely on various instruments. Listen carefully to the effect on your registrations. Use your discretion in adding this element.

5. Special Effects also vary widely on various instruments. If your instrument has an array of Special Effects, these can be used to enhance different compositions. Special Effects may include arpeggiators, chimes, reiterated sounds (banjo, mandolin, marimba, xylophone, etc.), synthesized sounds, percussion, and many others. Consult your owner's guide for directions in their use.

6. If your instrument has a Rhythm Unit, it can be used to advantage. Set it to the appropriate rhythms (waltz, swing, ballad, Latin, march, rock, etc.). Adjust the tempo setting to a realistic pulse — one in which you can play comfortably. With the Rhythm Unit on, look through the piece to make sure the flash comes immediately AFTER the bar line (on the down beat). This will give you a better understanding of the flow of the pulse and will prepare you to begin practice.

7. Create a NEW registration for every piece. Begin to give more thought to imaginative registrations. Repeat previously learned pieces trying new registrations (write them in pencil). Experiment with registrations in new pieces.

HALF STEPS AND WHOLE STEPS

HALF STEP

From one key to the nearest key with NO KEY IN BETWEEN is a HALF STEP.

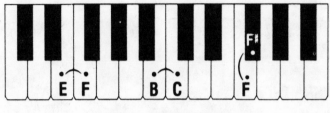

HALF STEPS (1/2)

WHOLE STEP

From one key to a neighbor key with ONE KEY IN BETWEEN is a WHOLE STEP.

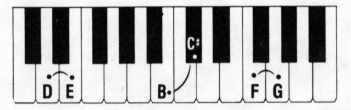

WHOLE STEPS (1)

C MAJOR SCALE

HOW MAJOR SCALES ARE FORMED

The word SCALE comes from a Latin word meaning LADDER. A scale has tones (like steps on a ladder) which go up and down. There are eight tones in a Major scale. The tones are called scale DEGREES. The scale degrees are arranged in the pattern of WHOLE STEPS (1) and HALF STEPS (½) shown below:

C MAJOR SCALE

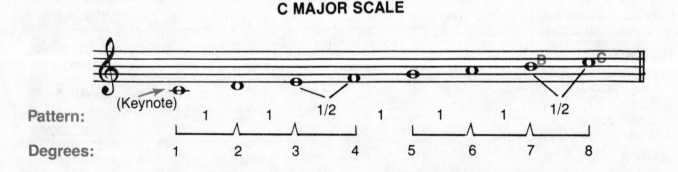

Pattern: (Keynote)   1   1   1/2   1   1   1   1/2

Degrees: 1   2   3   4   5   6   7   8

Scale Preparation Drills

TURNING THE THUMB UNDER

PRACTICE DIRECTIONS
Practice these drills for turning the THUMB UNDER. Play each drill several times. Practice SLOWLY at first.

CROSSING OVER THE THUMB

PRACTICE DIRECTIONS
Practice these drills for crossing OVER THE THUMB. Play each drill several times. Practice SLOWLY at first.

Harmonizing the C Major Scale

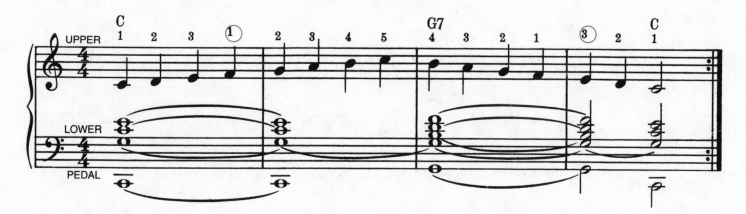

*For additional scale practice using both hands, see pages 45 and 95.

Scale Melodies

PRACTICE DIRECTIONS
Many songs use scales in their melodies. Several Christmas songs are given below. Play each song with your Right Hand.

ALL ORGANS
Choose any suitable registration.

UPPER:_____

THE FIRST NOEL

The__ first _____ No - el the __ an - gels did say,

JOY TO THE WORLD

Joy to ____ the world! The Lord is come.

AWAY IN A MANGER

A - way___ in a man - ger, no crib for a bed,

IT CAME UPON THE MIDNIGHT CLEAR

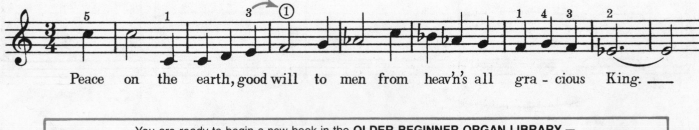

Peace on the earth, good will to men from heav'n's all gra - cious King. __

You are ready to begin a new book in the **OLDER BEGINNER ORGAN LIBRARY —
Great Christmas Carols, Level 1.**

TIME SIGNATURE $C = \frac{4}{4}$

The sign **C** is another way of indicating the $\frac{4}{4}$ time signature. This sign is called COMMON TIME.

ELECTRONIC ORGANS
UPPER: Reed Solo (Oboe, Saxophone, Clarinet) 8′
LOWER: Diapason 8′
PEDAL: 8′
TREM. and VIB: Off

DRAWBAR ORGANS
No. 4

C MAJOR SCALE ETUDE*

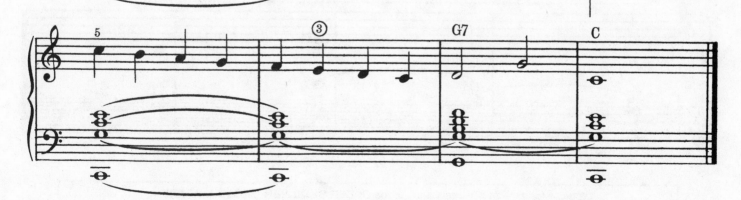

*ETUDE (pronounced "ay-tood") is a French word meaning STUDY or EXERCISE.

ELECTRONIC ORGANS
UPPER: Piano or Flutes 8' 4'
LOWER: Diapason 8'
PEDAL: 8'
TREM. and VIB: Off

DRAWBAR ORGANS
UPPER: 00 8020 000
LOWER: (00) 4321 0000
PEDAL: 0 3 Spinet 3
VIB: Off
SPECIAL EFFECTS: Piano on Upper

COUNTRY GARDENS

OLD ENGLISH DANCE

You are ready to begin a new book in the **OLDER BEGINNER ORGAN LIBRARY** —
Great Hymns, Level 1.

TIME SIGNATURE $\mathbb{C} = \frac{2}{2}$

This sign $\mathbb{C}$ means ALLA BREVE (or "Cut Time"). There are TWO strong beats to the measure. When you first play in Cut Time, count $\frac{4}{4}$ (4 beats to the measure). Then, when you know the piece better, count $\frac{2}{2}$ time (2 beats to the measure).

ELECTRONIC ORGANS
UPPER: Flute 8′ String 8′ Trumpet 8′
LOWER: Diapason 8′ Flute 8′
PEDAL: 16′ 8′ String Bass 8′
TREM: On (Fast)
VIB: Off
RHYTHM: Fox Trot

DRAWBAR ORGANS
No. 5
RHYTHM: Fox Trot

CAN-CAN

JACQUES OFFENBACH
(1819-1880)

(*Melody 8va on repeat*)

REVIEW — UNIT 5

1. Write ½ under the half steps shown on this keyboard.

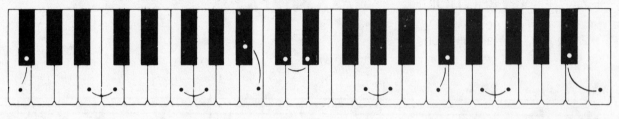

_____   _____   _____   _____   _____   _____   _____   _____

2. Write 1 under the whole steps shown on this keyboard.

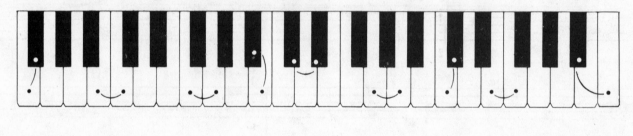

_____   _____   _____   _____   _____   _____   _____   _____

3. How many tones are there in a Major scale? _____ .

4. The tones are called scale _____ .

5. Mark the whole (1) and half (½) steps in this C Major scale.

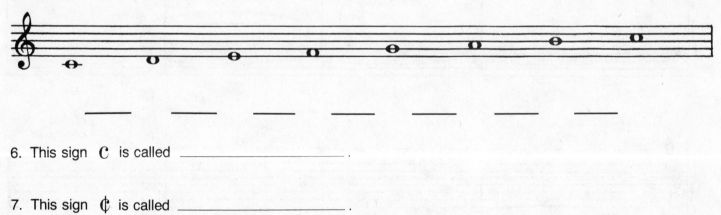

_____   _____   _____   _____   _____   _____   _____

6. This sign C is called _____ .

7. This sign ₵ is called _____ .

UNIT 6

- **G MAJOR FIVE FINGER POSITION**
- **D7 CHORD**
- **DOTTED RHYTHM**
- **G MAJOR SCALE**

PRACTICE DIRECTIONS

Play the C Major scale with your Left Hand. Also, play the C Major scale on the pedals with your Left Foot. Play the pedal notes one octave (eight notes) lower than written.

C Major Scale for the Left Hand and Pedals

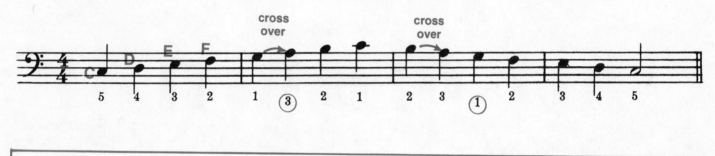

INTERVALS

The distance in pitch between two notes is called an INTERVAL.

PRACTICE DIRECTIONS

1. Hold (tie) the lowest note throughout.
2. Use FINGER SUBSTITUTIONS (changing fingers while holding down a key) to play out of the five finger position.
3. Play first with your Right Hand, then with your Left Hand. Play the Left Hand one octave (eight notes) lower than written.

Interval Exercise*

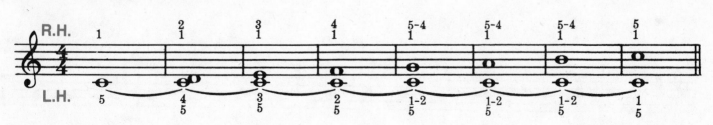

*See page 91 for more exercises of this type.

G MAJOR KEY SIGNATURE

The sharps or flats at the beginning of each staff tell you the KEY SIGNATURE. (Exception: the key of C Major has NO sharps or flats.)

The key signature tells you: 1) which notes to play sharped or flatted THROUGHOUT the piece, and
2) the main tonality or KEY of the piece.

SHARP key signatures are identified by:
1) naming the last sharp, then

2) naming the next letter in the musical alphabet (the name of the next note ABOVE the last sharp).

Key of G Major

G MAJOR FIVE FINGER POSITION

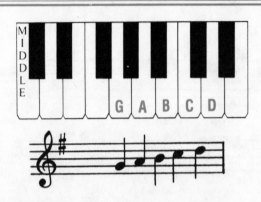

PRACTICE DIRECTIONS
1. Play the following **Warm-Up Drills** with your Right Hand. Name the notes aloud as you play. MEMORIZE them.*
2. Play the same drills with your Left Hand one octave lower than written. Name the notes aloud as you play.

Warm-Up Drills

Key of G Major

1.

R.H.

L.H.

2.

R.H.

L.H.

*Drill on these notes using the **Bastien Music Flashcards.**

D7 CHORD

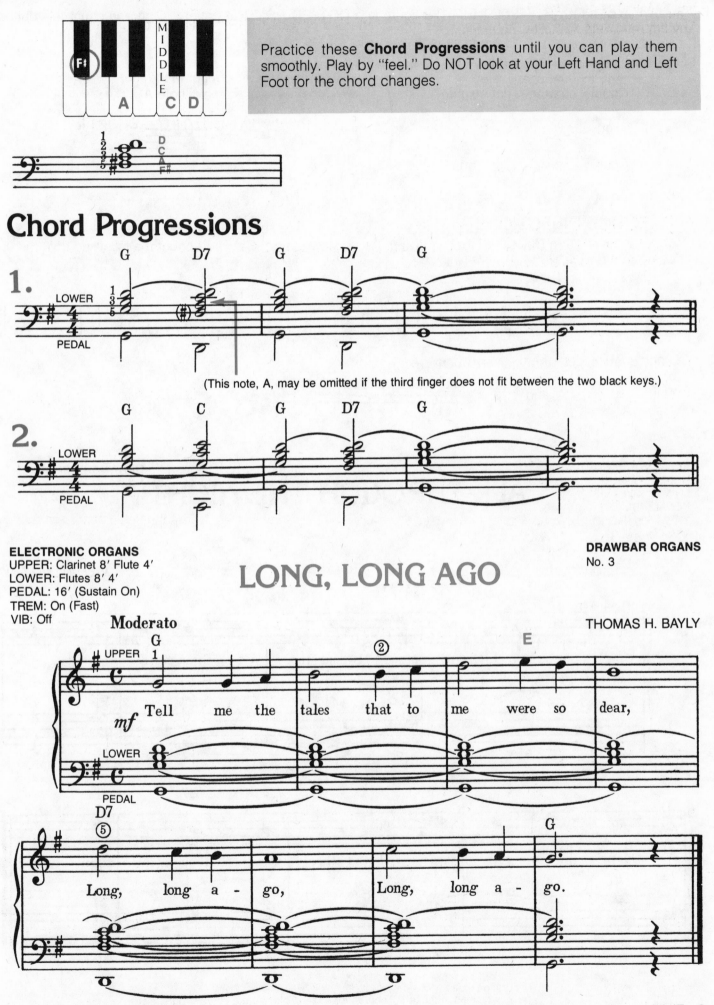

Practice these **Chord Progressions** until you can play them smoothly. Play by "feel." Do NOT look at your Left Hand and Left Foot for the chord changes.

Chord Progressions

1.

(This note, A, may be omitted if the third finger does not fit between the two black keys.)

2.

ELECTRONIC ORGANS
UPPER: Clarinet 8′ Flute 4′
LOWER: Flutes 8′ 4′
PEDAL: 16′ (Sustain On)
TREM: On (Fast)
VIB: Off

LONG, LONG AGO

DRAWBAR ORGANS
No. 3

THOMAS H. BAYLY

Moderato

Tell me the tales that to me were so dear,

Long, long a - go, Long, long a - go.

DOTTED RHYTHM

The rhythm of a QUARTER-DOT EIGHTH figure is a DOTTED RHYTHM pattern. Clap and count this dotted rhythm pattern in the following manner:

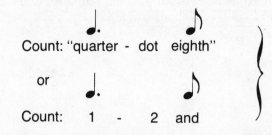

Count: "quarter - dot eighth"

or

Count: 1 - 2 and

This rhythm has a LONG — SHORT feel.

PRACTICE DIRECTIONS

Turn on the Rhythm Unit to Fox Trot or Swing. Use a slow tempo. Clap and count the following rhythm aloud to the beat of the Rhythm Unit.

Count: "quarter - dot   8th quarter quarter
or
Count: 1 - 2   and 3   4

ELECTRONIC ORGANS
UPPER: Flutes 8′ 4′
LOWER: String 8′
PEDAL: 16′
TREM: On (Fast)
VIB: On (Full)
RHYTHM: Fox Trot or Swing

DRAWBAR ORGANS
No. 11
RHYTHM: Fox Trot or Swing

ALL THROUGH THE NIGHT

Andante

WELSH LULLABY

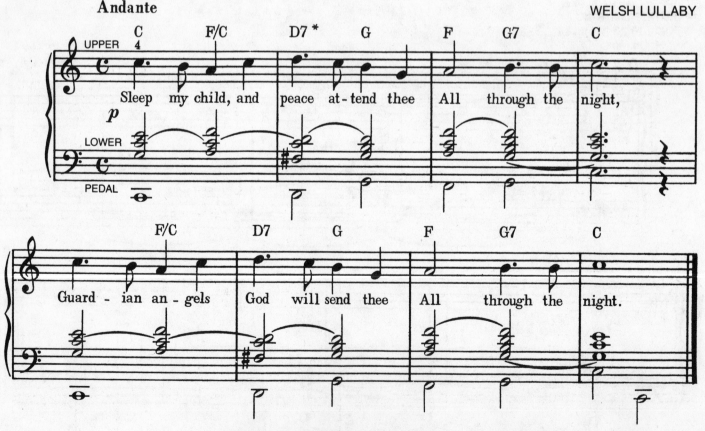

*The A is omitted in these D7 chords for ease in playing the chord progressions.

G MAJOR SCALE

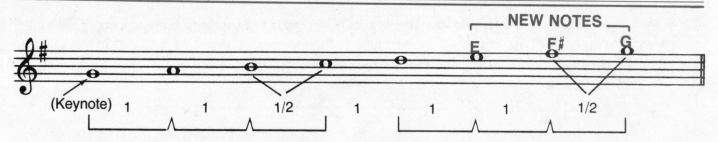

NEW NOTES

E   F#   G

(Keynote)   1   1   1/2   1   1   1   1/2

PRACTICE DIRECTIONS
First play the G Major scale with your Right Hand alone. Next, play the G Major scale with the accompaniment.

Harmonizing the G Major Scale

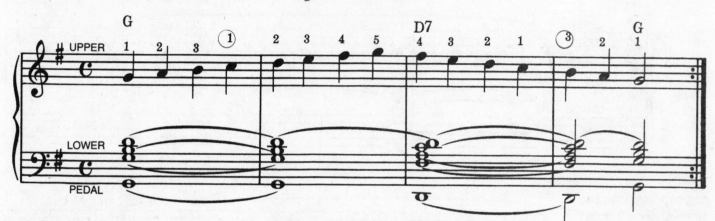

ELECTRONIC ORGANS
UPPER: Flutes 16′ 8′ 4′ Strings 16′ 8′ 4′
LOWER: Diapason 8′
PEDAL: Tibia 16′ Flute 8′ (Sustain On)
TREM: On (Fast)
VIB: Off
RHYTHM: March (4/4)

MICHAEL, ROW THE BOAT ASHORE

DRAWBAR ORGANS
No. 1
RHYTHM: March (4/4)

With spirit

SPIRITUAL

Mi-chael row the boat a - shore, Al - le - lu -

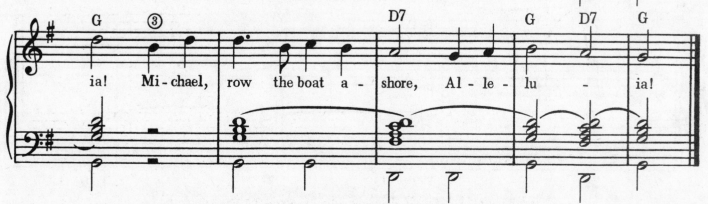

ia! Mi - chael, row the boat a - shore, Al - le - lu - ia!

SLUR

A SLUR is a curved line over or under notes of DIFFERENT pitches. The notes within the slur line are to be played legato (smooth and connected).

PHRASE

A PHRASE is a musical sentence. Slurs are used to indicate the beginning and end of the phrase (musical thought).

ELECTRONIC ORGANS
UPPER: Flutes 8′ 4′ 2′ Strings 8′ 4′
LOWER: Diapason 8′ Flute 8′ Reed 8′
PEDAL: 16′ 8′
TREM: On (Slow/Celeste)
VIB: Off

HYMN TUNE

DRAWBAR ORGANS
No. 2

from "KATHOLISCHES GESANGBUCH"
PETER RITTER

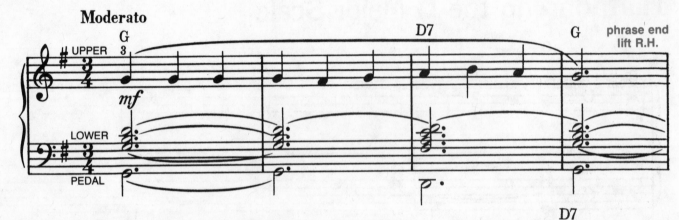

D.S. AL FINE

D. S. al Fine (abbreviation for *Dal Segno al Fine*) is a DIRECTION sign. It means to go back to the sign (𝄋) and play to the word *"Fine."*

PRACTICE DIRECTIONS

1. Practice the pedal part first. Turn on the Rhythm Unit to Rock, using a slow tempo. Play the pedal part to the beat of the Rhythm Unit.
2. Practice the pedal part and the Left Hand chords together.
3. Practice the melody alone. Learn one phrase at a time.
4. Finally play as written. (If the pedal part is too difficult, play one pedal G at the beginning of each measure.)

ELECTRONIC ORGANS
UPPER: Flutes 8′ 2′
       (or Flutes 16′ 4′ played 8va)
LOWER: Flute 8′ String 8′
PEDAL: String Bass (Sustain On)
TREM. and VIB: Off
RHYTHM: Rock

DRAWBAR ORGANS
No. 4
RHYTHM: Rock

THINKIN' 'BOUT YOU

*The same pedal note is played throughout the chord changes.

REVIEW — UNIT 6

1. Write the G Major key signature in both clefs.

2. Mark the whole (1) and half (½) steps in this G Major scale.

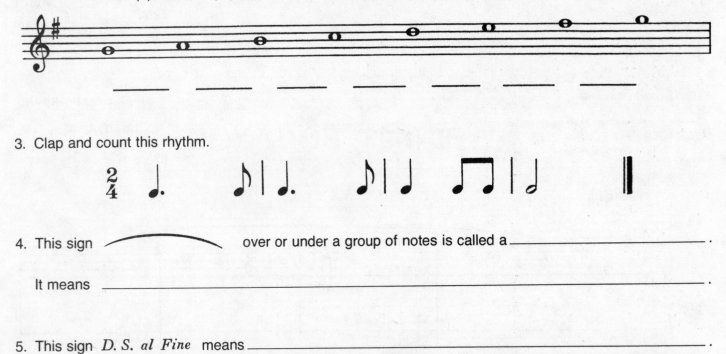

3. Clap and count this rhythm.

4. This sign _____ over or under a group of notes is called a _____.

   It means _____.

5. This sign *D. S. al Fine* means _____.

6. In front of each note draw the accidentals indicated. Play them.

7. Play the following chord progression with your Left Hand in the rhythm indicated.

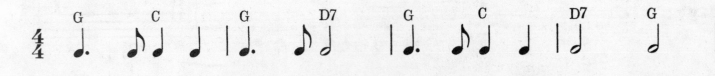

UNIT 7

- F MAJOR FIVE FINGER POSITION
- B♭ MAJOR CHORD
- C7 CHORD
- RHYTHM PATTERN — WALTZ TIME
- F MAJOR SCALE

FIRST AND SECOND ENDINGS

FIRST AND SECOND ENDINGS are used as space saving devices.

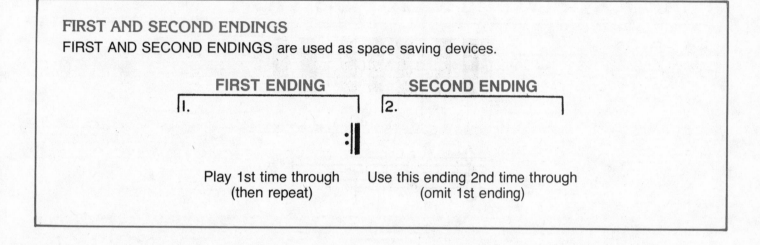

FIRST ENDING	SECOND ENDING
1.	2.
Play 1st time through (then repeat)	Use this ending 2nd time through (omit 1st ending)

ALL ORGANS
Using Registration No. 2 as a guide, write (in pencil) a registration of your choice.*

UPPER:_____

LOWER: _____

PEDAL:_____

TREM. or VIB:_____

Key of _____

SAINT ANTHONY CHORALE

JOSEPH HAYDN
(1732-1809)

*Refer to the **SUGGESTED ORGAN REGISTRATIONS** on the inside back cover.

F MAJOR KEY SIGNATURE

The key of F Major has one flat: B flat.
In a piece with an F Major key signature, play all the B's flatted.

F MAJOR FIVE FINGER POSITION

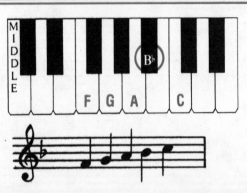

PRACTICE DIRECTIONS
1. Play the following **Warm-Up Drills** with your Right Hand. Name the notes aloud as you play. MEMORIZE them.*
2. Play the same drills with your Left Hand one octave lower than written. Name the notes aloud as you play.

Warm-Up Drills

Key of F Major

*Drill on these notes using the **Bastien Music Flashcards**.

B♭ MAJOR CHORD

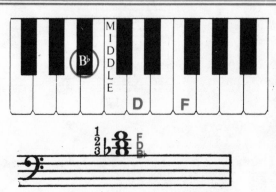

Practice the **Chord Progressions** on this page until you can play them smoothly. Play by "feel." Do NOT look at your Left Hand and Left Foot for the chord changes.

Chord Progression

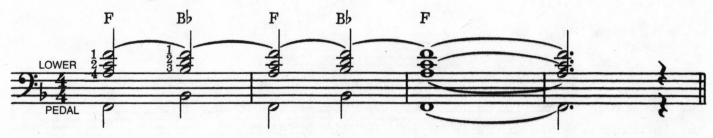

C7 CHORD

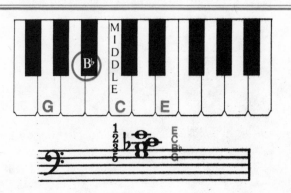

Chord Progressions

1.

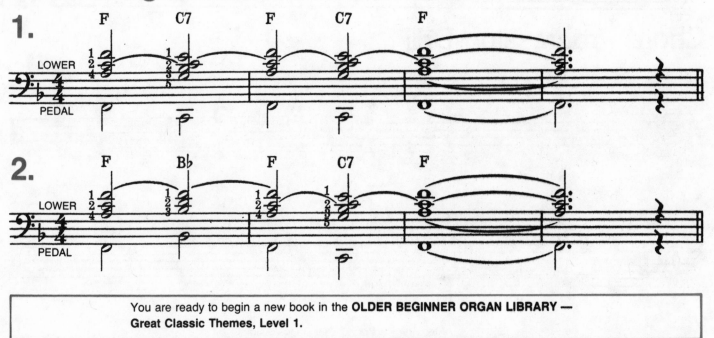

2.

You are ready to begin a new book in the **OLDER BEGINNER ORGAN LIBRARY —**
Great Classic Themes, Level 1.

RHYTHM PATTERN — WALTZ TIME ($\frac{3}{4}$)

WALTZ TIME features a strong accent on the first beat of each measure followed by two weaker beats creating an "OOM - pah - pah" effect.

TECHNIC FOR PLAYING WALTZ TIME

The waltz rhythm is produced by playing the pedal on the first beat of each measure and playing the chords with your Left Hand on the second and third beats.

Waltz Rhythm

PRACTICE DIRECTIONS

1. Turn on the Rhythm Unit to Waltz (3/4). Adjust the tempo to Moderate. Listen to the steady "OOM - pah - pah" pattern.
2. Play the **Waltz Rhythm** shown above. Play the pedal and chords with a short, detached touch (called STACCATO).*
3. Practice the **Chord Progression Drill** shown below in the same manner. This chord progression uses all of the chords you have learned. Practice these chords in waltz rhythm until you can play them smoothly without hesitation.

Chord Progression Drill

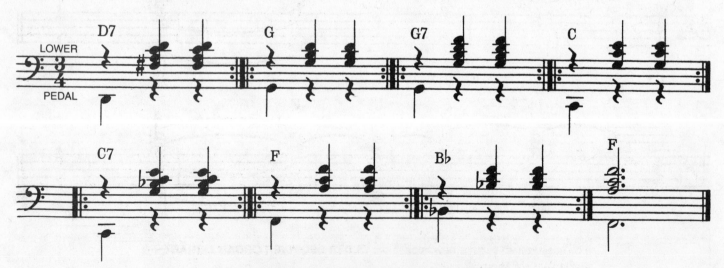

*See page 77 for examples of notated staccato signs.

ELECTRONIC ORGANS
UPPER: Diapason 8′ Flute 8′ Reed 8′
LOWER: Flutes 8′ 4′ String 8′
PEDAL: Bourdon 16′ Flute 8′ (Sustain On)
TREM: On (Fast)
VIB: On (Full)
RHYTHM: Waltz (3/4)

DRAWBAR ORGANS
No. 5
RHYTHM: Waltz (3/4)

DU, DU LIEGST MIR IM HERZEN

GERMAN FOLK SONG

Key of _____

F MAJOR SCALE

PRACTICE DIRECTIONS

Note the different Right Hand fingering used in the F Major scale. Practice this scale with your Right Hand.

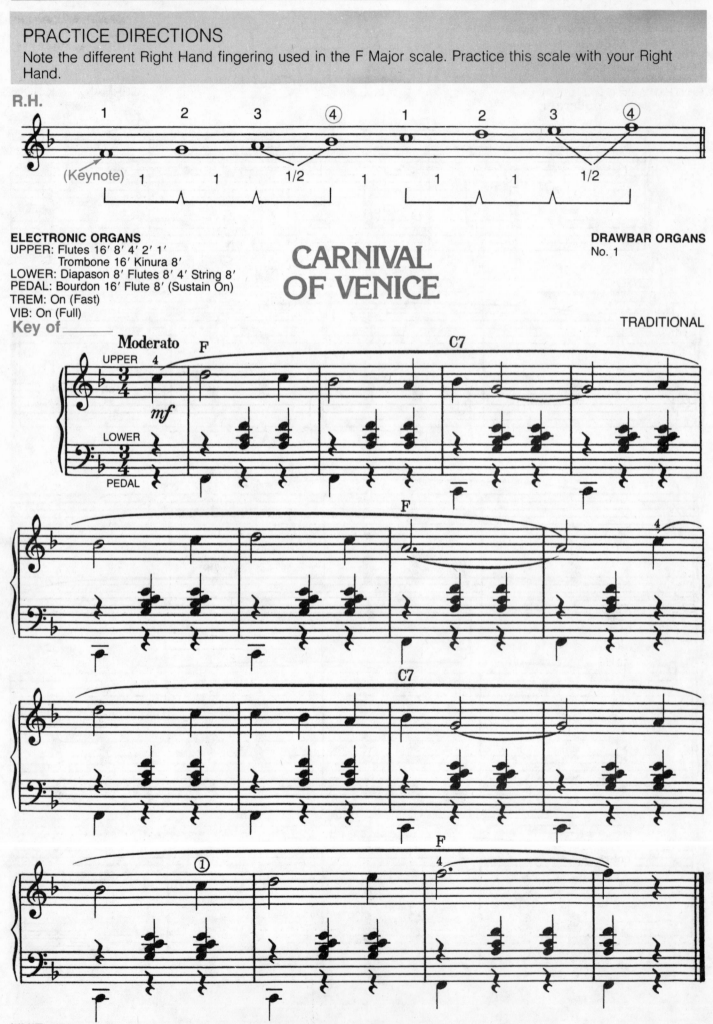

ELECTRONIC ORGANS
UPPER: Flutes 16' 8' 4' 2' 1'
       Trombone 16' Kinura 8'
LOWER: Diapason 8' Flutes 8' 4' String 8'
PEDAL: Bourdon 16' Flute 8' (Sustain On)
TREM: On (Fast)
VIB: On (Full)

DRAWBAR ORGANS
No. 1

CARNIVAL OF VENICE

TRADITIONAL

Key of _____

ELECTRONIC ORGANS
UPPER: Diapason 8' Flute 8' String 8'
       Oboe 8' Saxophone (or Kinura) 8'
LOWER: Flutes 8' 4' String 8'
PEDAL: Bourdon 16' Flute 8' (Sustain On)
TREM: Adjust to suit the piece
RHYTHM: Waltz (3/4)

DRAWBAR ORGANS
No. 5
RHYTHM: Waltz (3/4)

ON TOP
OF OLD SMOKY

FOLK SONG

Key of _____ Moderato

REVIEW — UNIT 7

1. Write the F Major key signature in both clefs.

2. Mark the whole (1) and half (1/2) steps in this F Major scale.

___ ___ ___ ___ ___ ___ ___

3. Name the Major key shown by each key signature.

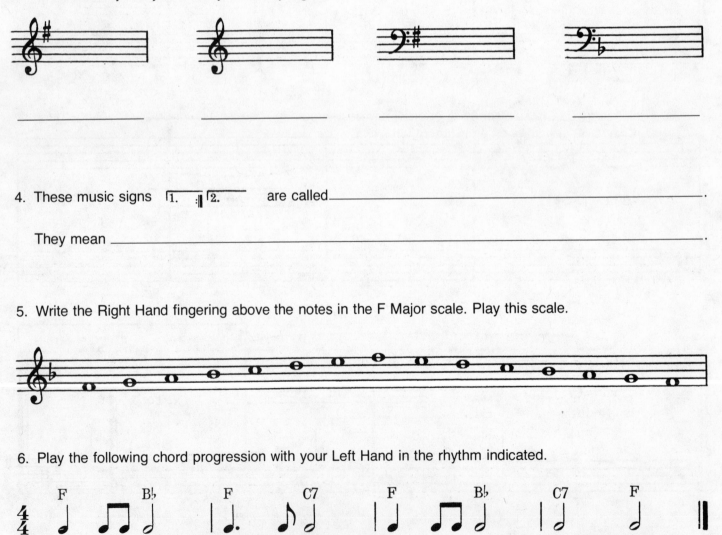

___ ___ ___ ___

4. These music signs $\boxed{1.}$:‖ $\boxed{2.}$ are called_____.

   They mean _____.

5. Write the Right Hand fingering above the notes in the F Major scale. Play this scale.

6. Play the following chord progression with your Left Hand in the rhythm indicated.

UNIT 8

- **MAJOR AND MINOR CHORDS**
- **INVERSIONS OF CHORDS**
- **GROUP 1 KEYS**
- **RHYTHM PATTERN — SWING TIME**

MAJOR AND MINOR CHORDS

Chords are built on scale degrees. The MAJOR TRIAD (3-note chord) built on the 1st tone of the Major scale is formed from 1st (Root), 3rd, and 5th tones of the scale. The triad is in ROOT POSITION when the 1st tone (Root) is the lowest note.

ROOT POSITION (FIRST POSITION)

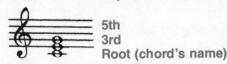

5th
3rd
Root (chord's name)

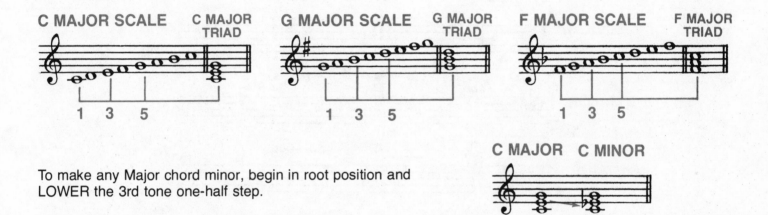

To make any Major chord minor, begin in root position and LOWER the 3rd tone one-half step.

PRACTICE DIRECTIONS

1. Practice these **Chord Drills.** The chords may be played hands separately or both hands together (on the same manual or on different manuals).
2. Play the root of each chord with the pedal. Hold it for both the Major and minor chords.

Chord Drills*

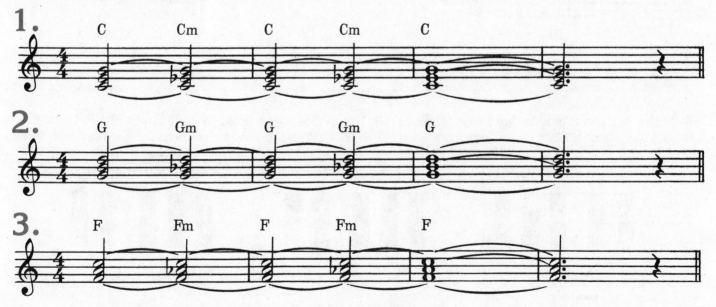

*For additional practice refer to pages 88 and 89 for other chords which may be practiced in this manner.

INVERSIONS OF CHORDS

Any ROOT POSITION triad may be INVERTED (rearranged) by moving the ROOT note to the TOP or MIDDLE. A triad has three possible positions:

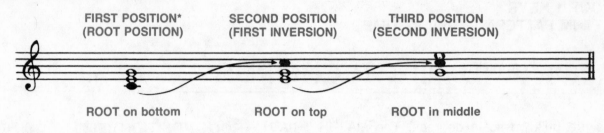

FIRST POSITION* (ROOT POSITION)	SECOND POSITION (FIRST INVERSION)	THIRD POSITION (SECOND INVERSION)
ROOT on bottom	ROOT on top	ROOT in middle

You have already played the C triad in Third Position, the G triad in First Position, and the F triad in Second Position:

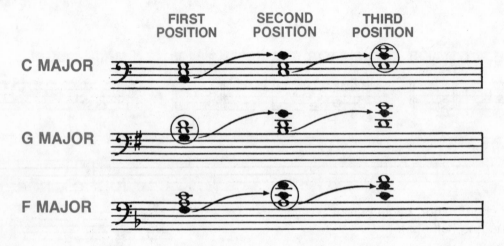

PRACTICE DIRECTIONS Practice these Major and minor chords in INVERTED positions.

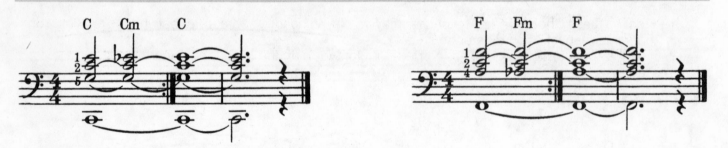

GROUP 1 KEYS (C, G, F)

You have learned to play in three keys: C, G, and F. These three keys are called the GROUP 1 KEYS because they all have the SAME feel and look in their FIRST POSITION chords. All three chords are formed with WHITE keys:

C MAJOR CHORD

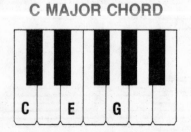

C E G

G MAJOR CHORD

G B D

F MAJOR CHORD

F A C

"white — white — white"

*These terms may be used interchangeably.

Preparatory Drill

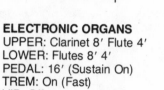

ELECTRONIC ORGANS
UPPER: Clarinet 8' Flute 4'
LOWER: Flutes 8' 4'
PEDAL: 16' (Sustain On)
TREM: On (Fast)
VIB: Off

DRAWBAR ORGANS
No. 3

BEAUTIFUL DREAMER

STEPHEN FOSTER

Key of _____ **Moderato**

1. Beau - ti - ful dream - er, wake un - to me,_____ Star - light and dew - drops are wait - ing for thee;_____
2. Sounds of the rude world head in the day,_____ Lull'd by the moon - light have all pass'd a - way._____

RHYTHM PATTERN — SWING TIME ($\frac{4}{4}$)

SWING TIME features strong accents on the first and third beats of each measure, creating an "OMM - pah - OOM - pah" effect.

TECHNIC FOR PLAYING SWING TIME
The swing rhythm is produced by playing the pedal on beats one and three of each measure and playing the chords with the Left Hand on beats two and four.

Swing Rhythm

> ## PRACTICE DIRECTIONS
> 1. Turn on the Rhythm Unit to Swing (Fox Trot, Ballad, etc.). Adjust the tempo to Moderate. Listen to the steady beat.
> 2. Play the **Swing Rhythm** shown above. Play the pedal and chords with a short, detached touch (called STACCATO*).
> 3. Practice the **Chord Progression Drill** shown below in the same manner. This chord progression uses most of the chords you have learned. Play each measure two or more times. Practice these chords in swing rhythm until you can play them smoothly without hesitation.

Chord Progression Drill

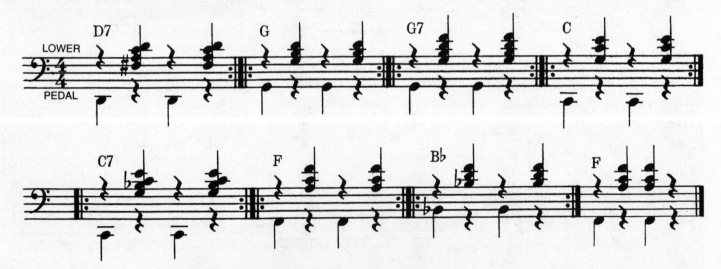

*Further explanation of STACCATO TOUCH is given on page 77.

ELECTRONIC ORGANS
UPPER: Flutes 16′ 8′ 4′ 2′ Reed 8′
LOWER: Diapason 8′ Flute 8′ String 8′
PEDAL: Bourdon 16′ Tibia 16′ Flute 8′
     (Sustain On)
TREM: On (Fast)
VIB: On (Full)

DRAWBAR ORGANS
No. 7

LITTLE BROWN JUG

Key of _____

TRADITIONAL

Lively

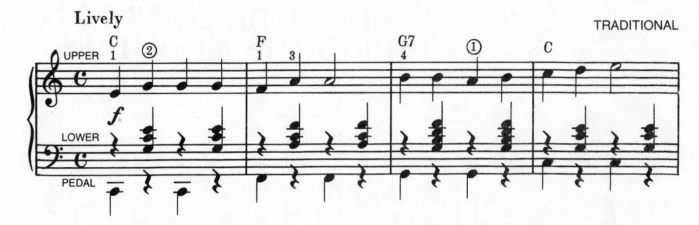

WALKING BASS

WALKING BASS is a technique of playing the pedal on the ROOT of a chord and "walking down" the scale. It is often used to "fill in" the bass part under a long melody note.

ELECTRONIC ORGANS
UPPER: Diapason 8′ Flute 8′ String 8′
      Oboe 8′ Saxophone 8′
      (or Kinura 8′)
LOWER: Flutes 8′ 4′ String 8′
PEDAL: Bourdon 16′ Flute 8′ (Sustain On)
TREM: On (Fast)
VIB: On (Full)
RHYTHM: March

DRAWBAR ORGANS
No. 5
VIB: On Full (V3)
RHYTHM: March

SHE'LL BE COMIN' ROUND THE MOUNTAIN

Bright march tempo

TRADITIONAL

REVIEW — UNIT 8

1. Write these key signatures in both clefs.

G MAJOR   **C MAJOR**   **F MAJOR**

2. To form a minor chord in root position, the _____ tone of the chord must be lowered one half step.

3. Name these minor chords. Play them.

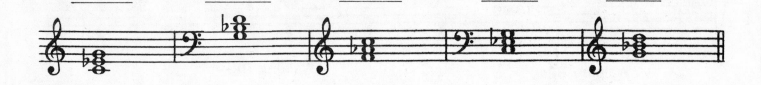

4. Play these chord progressions with your Left Hand and Left Foot.

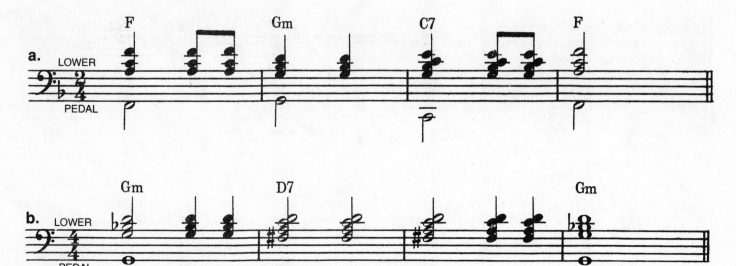

UNIT 9

- **PRIMARY CHORDS**
- **THE ORDER OF SHARPS**
- **MAJOR SHARP KEY SIGNATURES**
- **GROUP 2 KEYS**
- **READING IN D MAJOR**
- **READING IN A MAJOR**
- **READING IN E MAJOR**

PRIMARY CHORDS

I IV V

Chords are labeled with Roman numerals to indicate the degree of the scale on which each chord is formed.

The PRIMARY CHORDS are built on the 1st, 4th, and 5th degrees of the scale. Each scale degree has a name. The primary chord names are:

> **I - TONIC**
> **IV - SUB-DOMINANT**
> **V - DOMINANT**

V7 CHORD

You have played both the V chord and the V7 chord (DOMINANT SEVENTH). The dominant seventh is a 4-note chord. It is formed in root position by adding another note above the V chord. The V7 chord has a Root and the intervals of a 3rd, 5th, and 7th.

KEY OF C MAJOR (I=C)

DOMINANT
SEVENTH

V7 CHORD - INVERTED

You have played the V7 chord in root position and in inverted (rearranged) positions. (The inverted V7 chord is used in some keys for a better sound.)

THE ORDER OF SHARPS

The SHARPS are ALWAYS written in the same order on the staff. MEMORIZE this order.

LINE SHARP

SPACE SHARP

F C G D A E B

PRACTICE DIRECTIONS   Write the order of sharps three times on this staff.

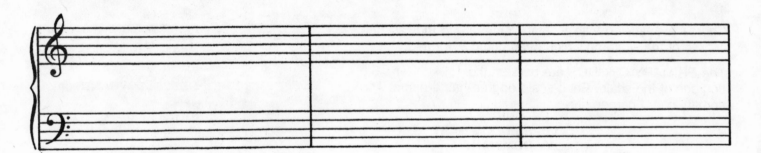

MAJOR SHARP KEY SIGNATURES*

The KEY SIGNATURE at the beginning of each staff tells you:
1) which notes to play sharped or flatted THROUGHOUT the piece
   and
2) the main tonality or KEY of the piece.

> **RULES FOR FINDING SHARP KEY SIGNATURES**
>
> 1) Name the LAST sharp to the right
>   then
> 2) name the NEXT letter in the musical alphabet (go UP a half step).
>   This is the name of the MAJOR KEY.

PRACTICE DIRECTIONS   Name these keys.

Example:

G   _____   _____   _____

*Drill on the sharp keys using the **Bastien Music Flashcards.***

GROUP 2 KEYS (D, A, E̲)

The GROUP 2 KEYS (D, A, E̲) have a BLACK KEY under the middle finger and white keys on either side in their FIRST POSITION I or tonic chords. E is underlined because it is the UNUSUAL Key in this group. The five finger position in E has TWO black keys in the middle.*

POSITIONS FOR THE GROUP 2 KEYS

PRACTICE DIRECTIONS

The circled finger numbers outline the I or tonic chords within the five finger positions below. Play these five finger positions and I chords. MEMORIZE them.

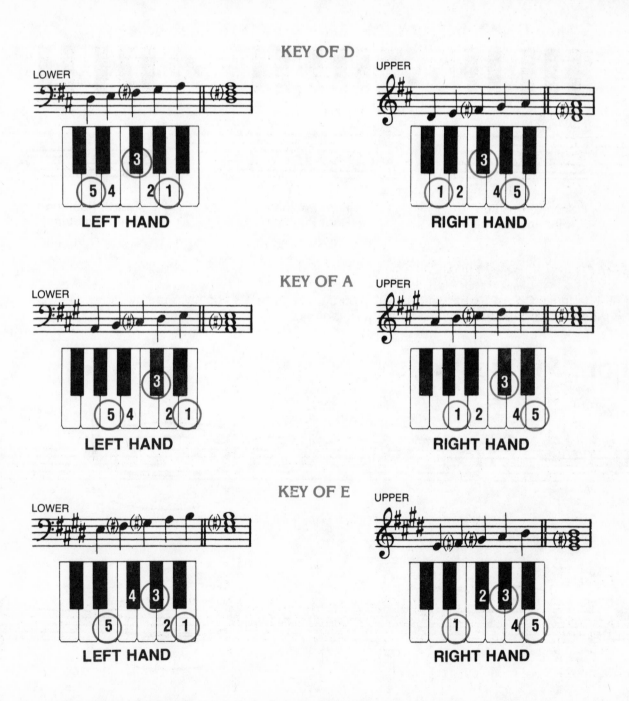

KEY OF D

LEFT HAND   RIGHT HAND

KEY OF A

LEFT HAND   RIGHT HAND

KEY OF E

LEFT HAND   RIGHT HAND

*Some organs may have keys of other colors. The black keys referred to here are "sharped" keys.

READING IN D MAJOR

FIVE FINGER POSITION*

PRIMARY CHORDS

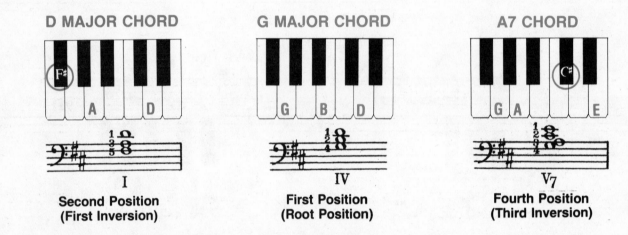

D MAJOR CHORD	G MAJOR CHORD	A7 CHORD
I	IV	V7
Second Position (First Inversion)	First Position (Root Position)	Fourth Position (Third Inversion)

Chord Progressions

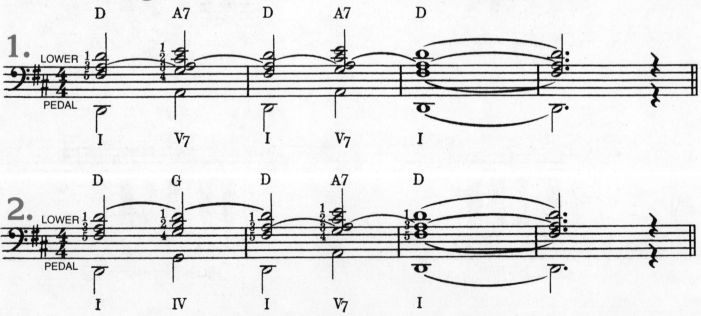

*The complete D Major scale is given on page 95.

ELECTRONIC ORGANS
UPPER: Flute 4'
LOWER: String 8'
PEDAL: Bourdon 16'
TREM: On (Slow/Celeste)
VIB: On (Light)
RHYTHM: Ballad or Other 4/4

KUM-BA-YA*

DRAWBAR ORGANS
No. 10
RHYTHM: Ballad

FOLK ANTHEM

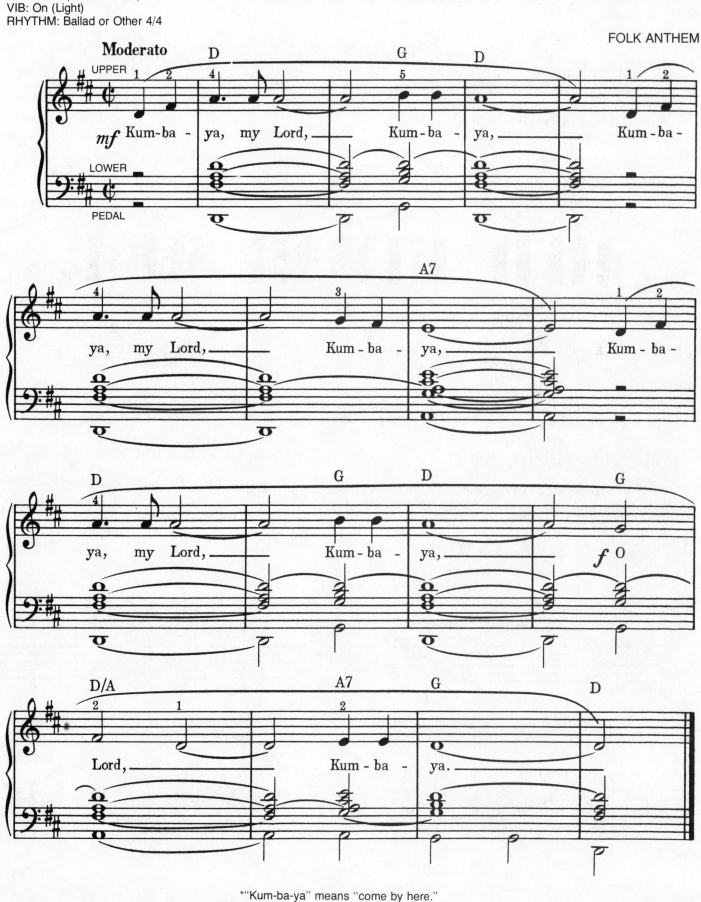

*"Kum-ba-ya" means "come by here."

READING IN A MAJOR

FIVE FINGER POSITION*

PRIMARY CHORDS

A MAJOR CHORD	D MAJOR CHORD**	E7 CHORD
I	IV	V7
First Position (Root Position)	**Third Position** (Second Inversion)	**Second Position** (First Inversion)

Chord Progressions

*The complete A Major scale is given on page 95.
**Note the different position of the D Major chord.

BOTH HANDS ON ONE MANUAL

The indication for playing both hands on the same manual is given with a bracket and the name of the manual to be used. This technique can be used, as in the **GERMAN FOLK SONG**, to create an echo effect.

LOWER

ELECTRONIC ORGANS
UPPER: Flutes 8′ 4′ Oboe 8′
LOWER: Flutes 8′ 4′
PEDAL: Tibia 16′ (Sustain On)
TREM: On (Slow/Celeste)
VIB: On (Light)
RHYTHM: Ballad or Swing

DRAWBAR ORGANS
No. 3
RHYTHM: Ballad

GERMAN FOLK SONG

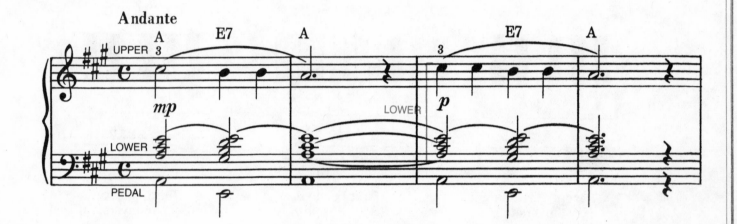

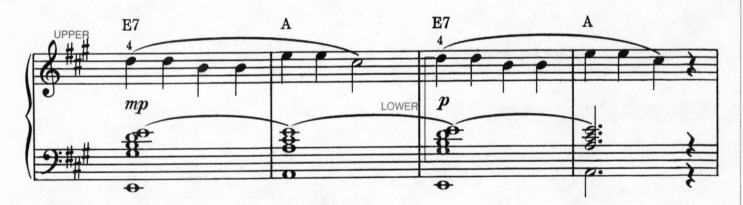

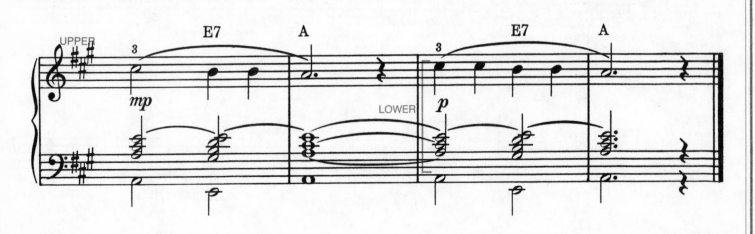

READING IN E MAJOR

FIVE FINGER POSITION*

PRACTICE DIRECTIONS

First, play the notes above with your Right Hand; then with your Left Hand (an octave lower than written); then on the pedals. Name the notes aloud as you play.

PRIMARY CHORDS

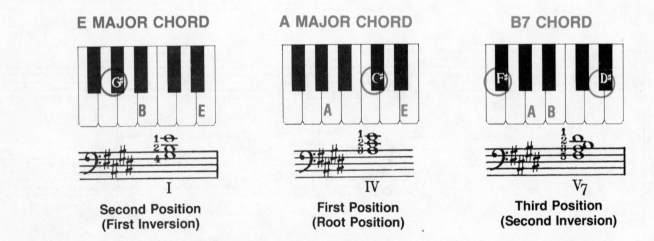

E MAJOR CHORD
Second Position
(First Inversion)
I

A MAJOR CHORD
First Position
(Root Position)
IV

B7 CHORD
Third Position
(Second Inversion)
V₇

PRACTICE DIRECTIONS

Practice these **Chord Progressions** until you can play them smoothly. Play by "feel." Do NOT look at your Left Hand and Left Foot for the chord changes.

Chord Progressions

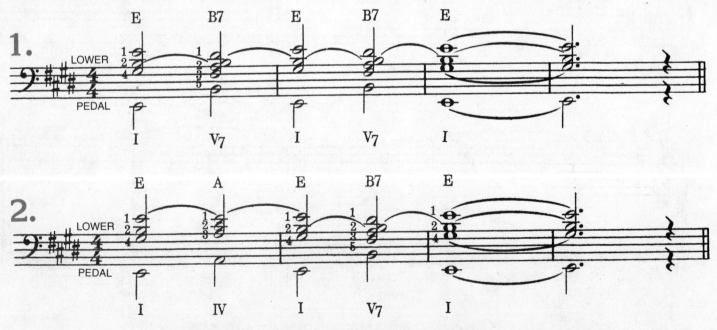

*The complete E Major scale is given on page 95.

STACCATO TOUCH

A DOT above or below a note means to play detached (short, separated). This is called STACCATO touch. Staccato is the opposite of legato.

ALL ORGANS
Using Registration No. 1 as a guide, write (in pencil) a registration of your choice.* (If you have a "Sustain" on the Upper Manual, use it.)

UPPER: _____
LOWER: _____
PEDAL: _____
TREM and VIB: Off
RHYTHM: (any 4/4)

CHA-CHA-CHA IN E

With spirit

*Refer to the **SUGGESTED ORGAN REGISTRATIONS** on the inside back cover.

REVIEW—UNIT 9

1. The order of sharps is _____ _____ _____ _____ _____ _____ _____.

2. Name these Major key signatures.

_____ _____ _____ _____

3. Write the I chords in root position for the Group 2 Keys. Play them.

4. What do they have in common? _____

5. These notes ♩ ♩ are played with a _____ touch.

6. Write the notes in each five finger position for the Group 2 Keys. Play them.

7. Which is the unusual key in Group 2? _____ Why? _____.

8. Name these Major and minor chords. Play them.

UNIT 10

- **ALTERNATING PEDALS**
- **GRADED DYNAMICS**

ALTERNATING PEDALS

Until now you have used the pedal mainly to play chord roots.

To add variation to the bass line both the root and 5th of the chord may be played alternately.

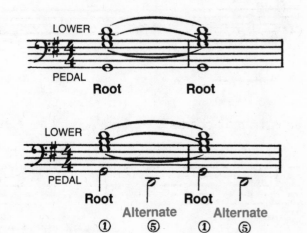

PRACTICE DIRECTIONS

Practice the patterns below using alternating pedals. Play each pattern several times. (From now on, as you learn each new chord, memorize its root and 5th alternate pedal)*

Pattern 1
Root played first.

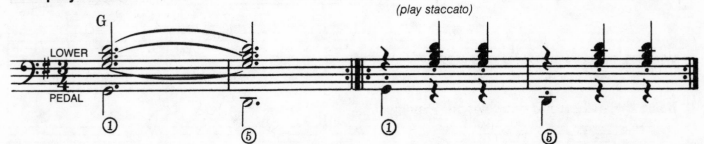

Pattern 2
Root or 5th played first.

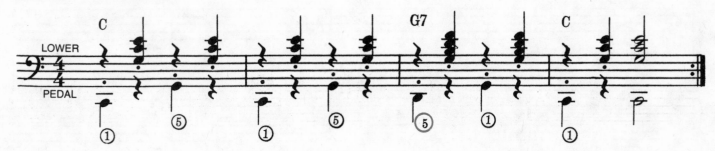

*For additional practice repeat previously learned pieces adding alternating pedals where appropriate.

ELECTRONIC ORGANS
UPPER: Diapason 8′ Flute 8′ String 8′
　　　Oboe 8′ Saxophone 8′ (or
　　　Kinura 8′)
LOWER: Flutes 8′ 4′ String 8′
PEDAL: Bourdon 16′ Flute 8′ (Sustain On)
TREM. and VIB: Adjust to suit the piece
RHYTHM: March (4/4)

THE CAISSONS
GO ROLLING ALONG

DRAWBAR ORGANS
No. 5 or No. 7
RHYTHM: March (4/4)

ARMY SONG
EDMUND L. GRUBER

Bright march tempo

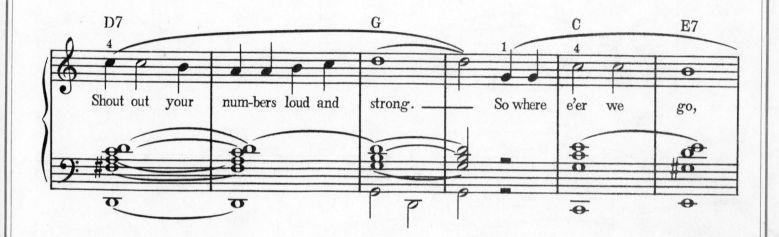

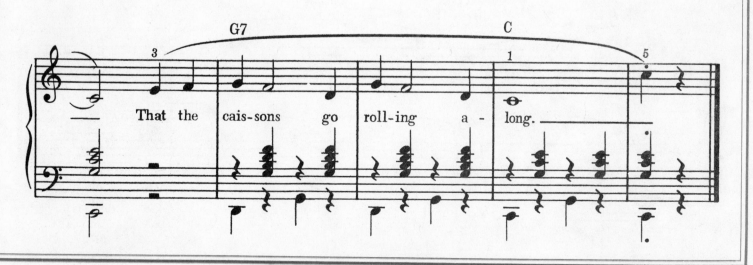

ELECTRONIC ORGANS
UPPER: Harpsichord (or Strings 8′ 4′)
LOWER: Flute 8′
PEDAL: Flute 8′
TREM: and VIB: Off

MINUET IN G

DRAWBAR ORGANS
No. 8

JOHANN SEBASTIAN BACH
(1685-1750)

GRADED DYNAMICS

GRADED DYNAMICS are gradual increases or decreases in the volume of sound.

The sign for increasing volume is ——————— or *cresc.* (the abbreviation for crescendo).

The sign for decreasing volume is ——————— or *decresc.* (the abbreviation for decrescendo)

or *dim.* (the abbreviation for diminuendo).

PRACTICE DIRECTIONS

1. Play a single tone or chord, gradually opening (press toe forward) and closing (press heel down) the Expression Pedal to produce the crescendo and decrescendo effect. Depress the toe or heel GRADUALLY without any sudden bursts of sound. (Opening and closing the pedal suddenly is used only for special effects.)
2. First, play only the melody of **FLOW GENTLY, SWEET AFTON**, observing the dynamic indications. Then, play again, adding the accompaniment.

ELECTRONIC ORGANS
UPPER: Clarinet 8′ Flute 4′
LOWER: Flutes 8′ 4′
PEDAL: 16′ (Sustain On)
TREM: On (Fast)
VIB: Off

FLOW GENTLY, SWEET AFTON

DRAWBAR ORGANS
No. 3

ROBERT BURNS
JAMES E. SPILMAN

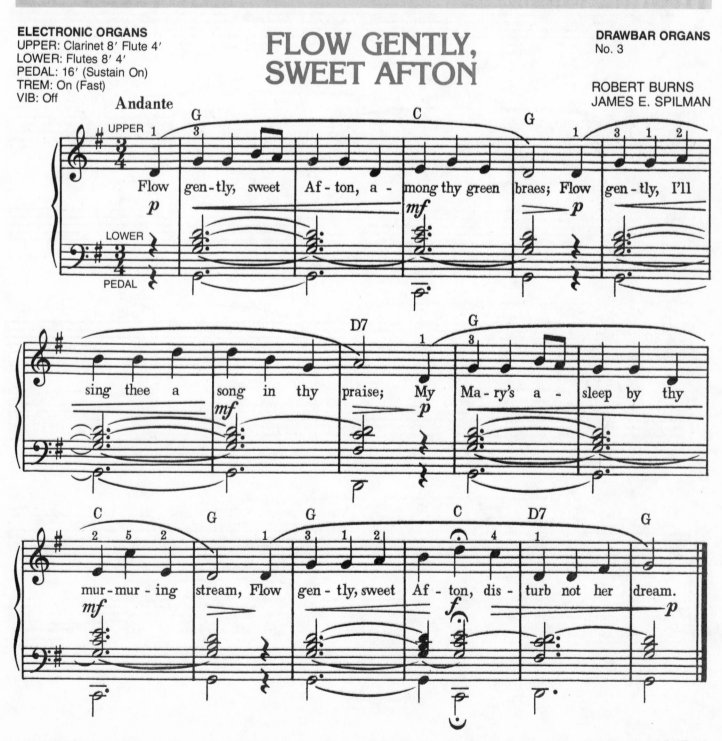

ELECTRONIC ORGANS
UPPER: Piano (or Flutes 8' 4')
LOWER: Diapason 8'
PEDAL: 16' 8' (Sustain On)
TREM. and VIB: Off

DRAWBAR ORGANS
SPECIAL EFFECT: Piano
or No. 4

THE ENTERTAINER

SCOTT JOPLIN
ARRANGED BY JAMES BASTIEN

Moderato

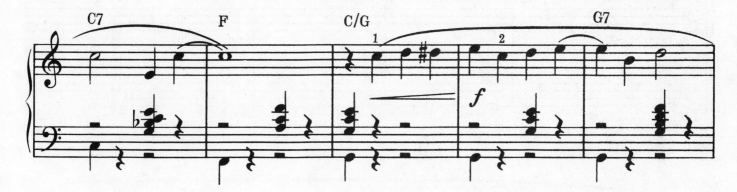

ELECTRONIC ORGANS
UPPER: Diapason 8′ Flute 8′ String 8′
        Oboe 8′ Saxophone 8′ (or
        Kinura 8′)
LOWER: Flutes 8′ 4′ String 8′
PEDAL: Bourdon 16′ Flute 8′ (Sustain On)
TREM. and VIB: Adjust to suit the piece

THE ASH GROVE

DRAWBAR ORGANS
No. 5

WELSH SONG

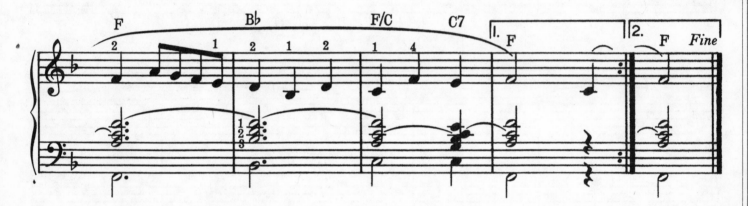

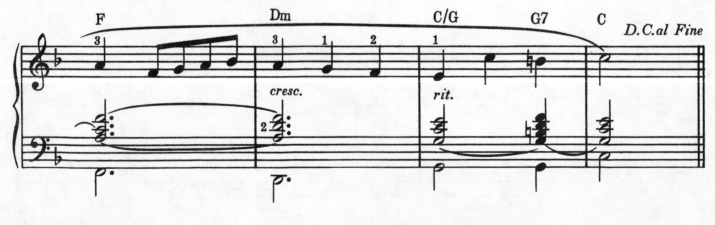

REVIEW—UNIT 10

1. Name these Major key signatures.

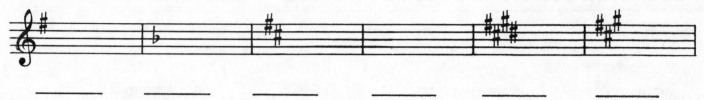

_____ _____ _____ _____ _____ _____

2. Write the pedal part in every other measure. Write a root and its alternate 5th. Play this accompaniment.

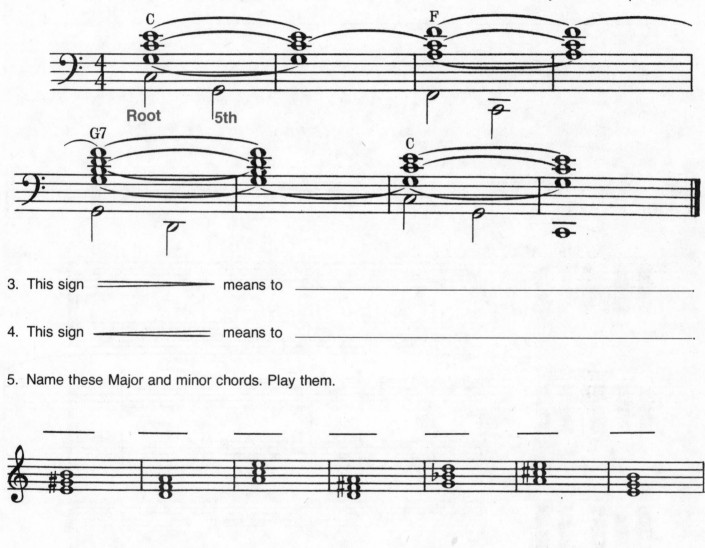

3. This sign ═══════ means to _____.

4. This sign ───────── means to _____.

5. Name these Major and minor chords. Play them.

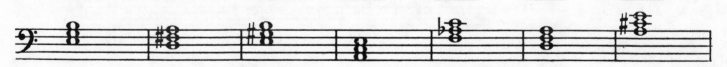

REFERENCE

FIVE FINGER POSITIONS AND I CHORDS

The twelve Major keys can be divided into four "position-related" groups according to their first position I or tonic chords.

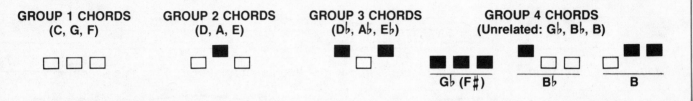

GROUP 1 CHORDS (C, G, F) **GROUP 2 CHORDS** (D, A, E) **GROUP 3 CHORDS** (D♭, A♭, E♭) **GROUP 4 CHORDS** (Unrelated: G♭, B♭, B)

G♭ (F♯)   B♭   B

PRACTICE DIRECTIONS

1. Practice these five finger positions and I chords. Learn one group of keys at a time. Memorize all four groups.
2. Lower the 3rd one-half step. Play the same four key groups in minor.
3. Practice again using this dotted rhythm:

GROUP 1 KEYS

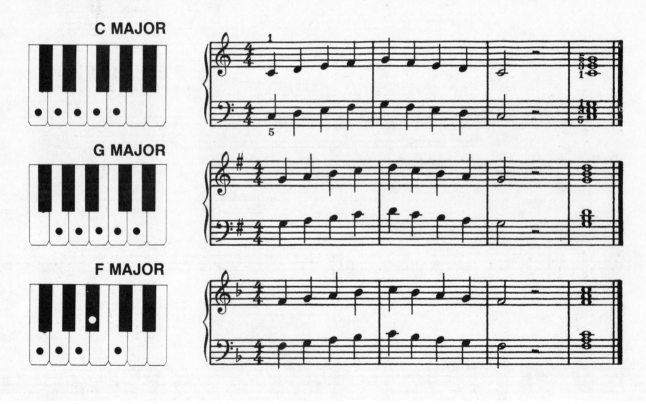

C MAJOR

G MAJOR

F MAJOR

GROUP 2 KEYS

D MAJOR

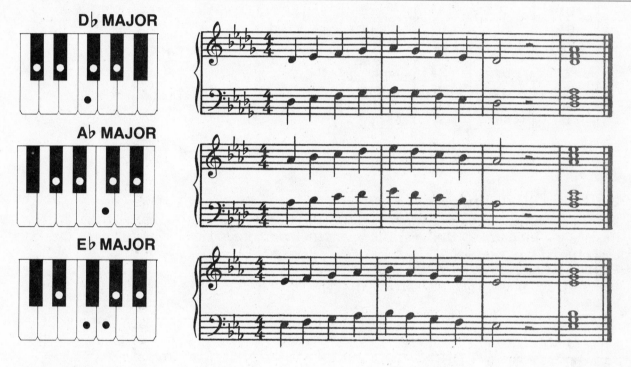

GROUP 3 KEYS

GROUP 4 KEYS

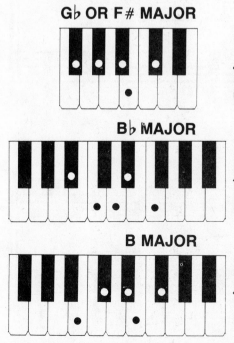

REFERENCE

CYCLE OF CHORD PROGRESSIONS

The twelve chords are arranged here to follow the natural order of chord progressions. The organist may begin with any chord and proceed clock-wise to succeeding chords.

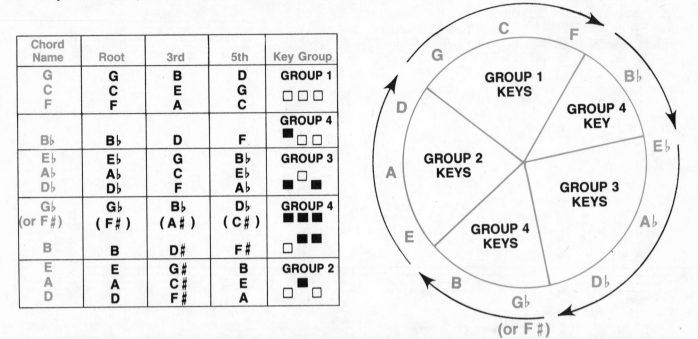

Chord Name	Root	3rd	5th	Key Group
G	G	B	D	**GROUP 1**
C	C	E	G	
F	F	A	C	
Bb	Bb	D	F	**GROUP 4**
Eb	Eb	G	Bb	**GROUP 3**
Ab	Ab	C	Eb	
Db	Db	F	Ab	
Gb (or F#)	Gb (F#)	Bb (A#)	Db (C#)	**GROUP 4**
B	B	D#	F#	
E	E	G#	B	**GROUP 2**
A	A	C#	E	
D	D	F#	A	

PRACTICE DIRECTIONS

1. Using the chart above, begin on any chord (**first** position) and proceed to the next chord in the cycle.
2. Practice the **Preparatory Drill** first as it is written. Then learn to play it in all the keys, following the cycle of chord progressions.
3. Practice the other three exercises in all keys.
4. Lower the 3rd of each chord one-half step. Play the same four exercises in minor.

1. PREPARATORY DRILL

2. WALTZ TIME

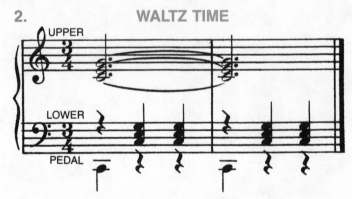

3. SWING TIME

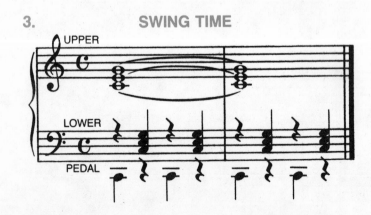

4. ALTERNATING PEDALS

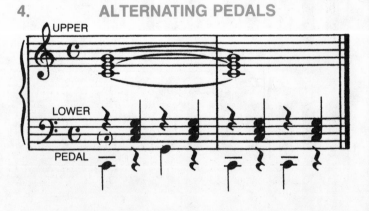

FINGER EXERCISES

FINGER SUBSTITUTION

The process of changing fingers on the same key is called FINGER SUBSTITUTION. In order to maintain a smooth legato line, often it is necessary to change fingers on the same key.

PRACTICE DIRECTIONS

1. Practice the exercise below first with the Right Hand as written. Repeat using the fingering 3-2 Repeat again using the fingering 4-3.
2. Play the Left Hand as written. Repeat using the fingering 2-3. Repeat again using the fingering 3-4.

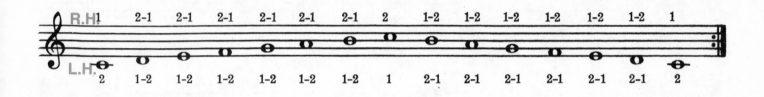

FINGER CROSSINGS

PRACTICE DIRECTIONS

1. Practice the exercise below first with the Right Hand as written. Repeat using the fingering 1-3. Repeat using the fingering 1-4.
2. Play the Left Hand as written. Repeat using the fingering 3-1. Repeat again using the fingering 4-1.

DOUBLE THIRDS

PRACTICE DIRECTIONS

Practice the exercise below first hands separately, then together. Use a legato touch.

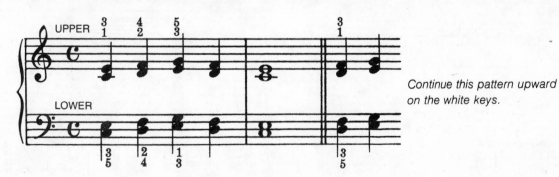

Continue this pattern upward on the white keys.

PEDAL EXERCISES

PRACTICE DIRECTIONS

1. Wear shoes! Position your Left Foot in line with G. Place your entire Right Foot on the Expression Pedal. Sit close enough to reach both C's easily. Position your knees together.
2. Keep your eyes on the music while playing each exercise.
3. Play, using the toe of your Left Foot. Use ankle motion only.
4. At the beginning, practice these pedal exercises no longer than five minutes at a time. Take a break before resuming pedal practice.

10. 4ths and 5ths

11.

12.

TRANSPOSITION

TRANSPOSITION is the process of playing or writing music in a different key from that in which it was originally written. (Notice the use of transposition in Pedal Exercise No. 12 above.)

PRACTICE DIRECTIONS

EVENING SONG is written below in C Major, G Major, and F Major as examples in transposition. First, play the melody in each key; then, add the chord accompaniment. For further practice in transposition, repeat several previously learned pieces (beginning at page 17) and transpose them into other keys.

EVENING SONG

Key of C

Key of G

Key of F

HANON STUDY

PRACTICE DIRECTIONS

1. Play the **HANON STUDY** with a legato touch.
2. Then, practice the same study in the four variations of touch and rhythm shown below.
3. While practicing, VARY THE TEMPO (practice three tempos: slow, medium, fast);
   VARY THE DYNAMICS (use the whole range of dynamics from soft to loud; use different registrations and the Expression Pedal);
   VARY THE KEY (transpose to other keys; remember to add the sharps or flats that belong to the key to which you are transposing).

CHARLES LOUIS HANON
(1820-1900)

FOUR VARIATIONS

STACCATO TOUCH

DOTTED RHYTHM

RHYTHM VARIANT — 1

RHYTHM VARIANT — 2

*Note the use of down stems for the Left Hand part when there is no pedal part written.

MAJOR SCALES

MUSIC DICTIONARY

TERM	ABBREVIATION or SIGN	MEANING
Alla Breve		$\frac{2}{2}$ time; two strong beats to the measure
Allegretto		moderately fast
Allegro		fast ("cheerful")
Andante		walking speed
A tempo		return to the original speed
Common Time	**C**	another way of indicating $\frac{4}{4}$ time
Crescendo	*cresc.* ⟍	gradually play louder
Da Capo al Fine	*D. C. al Fine*	return to the beginning and play to the word *"Fine"*
Decrescendo	*decresc.* ⟋	gradually play softer
Dal Segno al Fine	*D. S. al Fine*	return to the sign (𝄋) and play to the word *"Fine"*
Diminuendo	*dim.*	gradually play softer
Fermata	𝄐	hold the note (or notes) longer
Fine	*Fine*	the end
Forte	*f*	loud
Fortissimo	*ff*	very loud
Largo		very slowly
Legato		smooth, connected tones
Mezzo Forte	*mf*	moderately loud
Mezzo Piano	*mp*	moderately soft
Moderato		a moderate speed
Octave Sign	*8va*	play eight scale degrees (one octave) higher when the sign is above the notes; play eight scale degrees lower when the sign is below the notes
Pianissimo	*pp*	very soft
Piano	*p*	soft
Repeat Sign	𝄇	go back and play again
Ritardando	*rit.*	gradually play slower
Simile		similar
Staccato	♩̇	short, disconnected tones
Tempo		rate of speed
Tie	♩‿♩	connects notes on the same line or space; hold the notes for their combined value
Vivace		lively